EDITH SITWELL

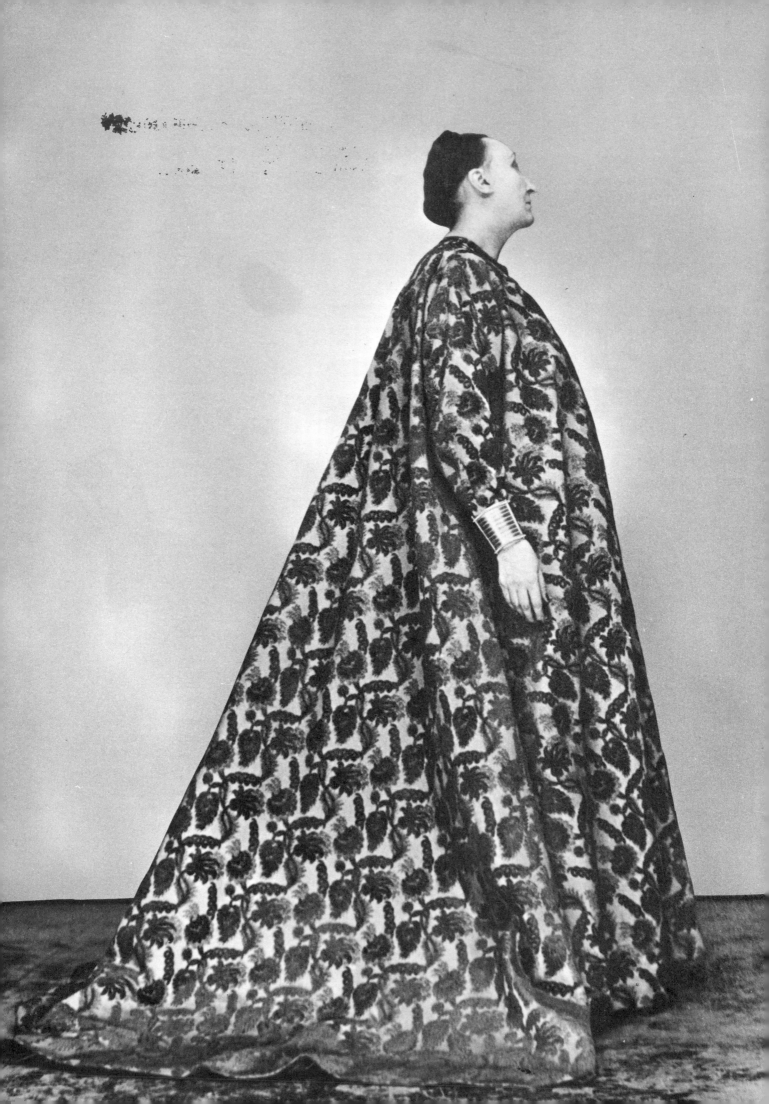

EDITH SITWELL

ELIZABETH SALTER

ORESKO BOOKS LTD·LONDON

(frontispiece)
Edith Sitwell in the sleep-walking scene from *Macbeth*. Photograph by George Platt Lynes.

ACKNOWLEDGEMENTS

The thanks of the publishers and the author are due in the first instance to Sir Sacheverell Sitwell, Mr. Reresby Sitwell and Mr. Francis Sitwell, without whose generous co-operation this book would not have been possible. They gave constant encouragement, provided many of the family photographs reproduced here for the first time and allowed the photography and reproduction of works of art in their private collections. The author also wishes particularly to thank Mr. Geoffrey Elborn and Dr. and Mrs. R. S. Bray for their assistance.

In addition sincere thanks are due to the following for providing photographs and giving permission for them to be reproduced:
Alinari, Florence; Associated Newspapers Group Ltd., London; Mrs. Jessie Bradley, Scarborough; Dr. and Mrs. R. S. Bray; British Library, Colindale, London; The Dowager Lady Camoys, Stonor Park, Oxfordshire; Mr. Howard Coster; *Country Life*, London; Mr. and Mrs. Donn Davies, Taos, New Mexico; Miss Paula Davies, London; Mr. Geoffrey Elborn, York; Mr. Mark Gerson, London; Leja Gorska; Gregory Harlip, London; The Cecil Higgins Art Gallery, Bedford; Humanities Research Center, University of Texas, Austin; The Edward James Foundation, Worthing; Mrs. Wyndham Lewis, Devonshire; Mander and Mitchison Theatre Collection, London; Mrs. Susana Guevara Mueller, Santa Barbara, California; National Portrait Gallery, London; Michael Parkin Fine Arts, London; George Platt Lynes, New York; Radio Times Hulton Picture Library, London; Scarborough Borough Council, Scarborough; Sheffield City Art Galleries, Sheffield; Sothebys Belgravia, London; Mr. Michael Stapleton, London; Mrs. A. Harper Statlender, La Roquette sur Siagne, France; Tate Gallery, London; Mr. Carl van Vechter, New York; Mr. Paul Walker, Sheffield City Polytechnic, Sheffield.
Whilst every effort has been made to clear copyright on photographs, this has not always been possible. The author and publishers apologize for any omissions that arise from this.

The extracts from Edith Sitwell's books and poetry and from Sir Osbert Sitwell's books are reproduced by permission of David Higham Associates Ltd., London.

For Michael Goodwin

First published in Great Britain in 1979 by
Oresko Books Limited, 167 Hermitage Road, London N4 1LZ.

ISBN 0 905368 50 9

Copyright © Elizabeth Salter 1979

Printed and bound in Great Britain by
JB Offset Printers (Marks Tey) Limited, Colchester, Essex.

EDITH SITWELL 1887-1964

For I was like one dead, like a small ghost,
A little cold air wandering and lost . . .

Whose body flat and strange, whose pale straight hair
Made me appear as though I had been drowned . . .

Edith Sitwell, 'Colonel Fantock'

SO EDITH SITWELL'S description of the child she was, first-born to that ill-matched couple, Sir George and Lady Ida Sitwell and alone for the first five years of her life. Her birth date was 7 September 1887 and photographs show that she was as round-faced and doll-pretty as most babies. The elongation of feature and body must have manifested itself in those early years, nevertheless, as she did not remember being regarded other than with dismay by either parent.

Her father, she said, had hoped for a daughter 'with a profile like a Pekingese dog and a taste for lawn tennis'. To her mother, who as a proud and beautiful seventeen-year-old had been forced, on family insistence, to enter into and remain within the bonds of matrimony, she was never other than a reminder of bondage. Consolation for Lady Ida came with the birth of Osbert, her first male child, adored from babyhood. It cannot have been coincidence that when her brother made his appearance the five-year-old 'Miss E', as she was known to the household, ran away from home, only to be returned by the policeman whom she had asked to help her button her boots. It was her one manifestation of jealousy. At no later stage of her life was Edith Sitwell other than protective of either Osbert or her younger brother Sacheverell. Osbert's arrival simply underlined her belief, fostered in those very early sensitive years, that she was a 'changeling', one who did not belong.

Her appearance, the chief cause of distress to both her parents, was in itself a statement of lineage. Her maternal grandmother was a Somerset, daughter of the duke of Beaufort, with a family tree that went back to the Tudors and beyond. Edith's colouring, the bone structure of her head and face, and the length and beauty of her hands showed a remarkable resemblance to Queen Elizabeth I. Like her mother she grew to be just under six feet tall but whereas the Lady Ida was an Italianate beauty, the child Edith was already a fledgling growing all too fast into 'the tall thin bird, wild and secretive with poetry' of her adolescence.

Her mental energy and, surprisingly, her taste for literature she inherited from Sir George, a baronet whose lineage did not compare with that of his wife but whose income resulted from the very considerable business ability shown by his ancestors. Unable to subdue the hostility of the unresponsive young beauty he had married, Sir George became an introvert whose concerns were mainly with history. Landscaping was his hobby and he wrote learnedly and with some grace on the subject of gardens. A great deal of his creative talent was spent on Renishaw, the family home in Derbyshire, but Edith's childhood memories were of the house at Wood End, 'dark and forgotten and a little precious like an unopened seventeenth-century first edition in a library'.

Much of her time was spent with her two grandmothers, Lady Londesborough, 'beaked like a harpy' with the 'queer roofed Byzantine eyes' that were inherited by her granddaughter, and the Dowager Lady Sitwell, that 'lady bountiful' whose charity Edith helped to distribute. Lady Londesborough she described as 'living in luxury like a gilded and irascible wasp in a fine ripe nectarine'. A formidable personage, she was queen of her domain. Travelling with her was an event. Liveried attendants would accompany her coach and, when she returned from a visit, a carpet would be unrolled so that her ladyship's shoes would be protected from contact with the earth. Only her butler and her personal servant were considered worthy of address. All instructions were given through them. Nor would any other member of her household be permitted to address her.

The child Edith was especially awed by the ceremony of de-wigging which took place each night.

A story she liked to tell was of the never-to-be-forgotten occasion when her grandmother, resplendent in a new white wig and surrounded by 'a frieze of captive daughters', was seated outside the gates of her garden. Unfortunately it happened to be Guy Fawkes' day and the local curate threw a penny into her lap. The outrage of the tempestuous Lady Londesborough can be imagined. Bent on the pursuit of health, 'that *magie bourgeoise*', she sent her granddaughter to be taken for walks beside the sea in the company of her aunts, 'tall as pagodas' with 'curls like bells of the blackest coral' under their sailor hats.

Miss E., who was of an affectionate disposition, looked for objects on whom she could lavish her love and chose Davis, her nurse, Dido, her dog, and 'Peaky', a peacock whom she admired because he was beautiful and wore a crown and with whom she walked through her father's garden with her head the height of his and her arm around his long and bejewelled neck. These were her companions until Osbert was old enough to be captive audience to her poetry readings, joined later by Sacheverell, the youngest. The alien being found that her enthusiasms were shared by her brothers and never afterwards felt herself to be so much alone. But they were too young to be of much help in the schoolroom in which a succession of governesses did their best to convert this girl, whose childish ambition was to be a genius, into an ordinary being.

Miss E. fought what she was later to describe as 'the loving, peering, inquisitive, interfering, middle class suffocation' but had to submit to her father's equally well-meant and even more painful interference with her bone structure. Observing the incipient curvature of her spine and the slightly crooked bridge of her nose, Sir George consulted a spine specialist. Between them they devised two iron frames into which Edith was manacled nightly. Her sufferings were as useless as the persuasions of her governess. Ordered to memorize such epics as 'The Boy Stood on the Burning Deck', the young Edith took a volume of Pope to bed with her and secretly and by candlelight memorized *The Rape of the Lock* instead. The curvature of the spine, though no doubt no worse, became no better. The long and slender nose never did become perfectly straight. Her sufferings were never forgotten.

There were compensations. Although no governess could induce her to exercise on the parallel bars, there was no difficulty in encouraging her to practise the piano. A teacher was procured for her and as her tastes were Romantic she learned Chopin and later Brahms. Her touch was delicate but, owing to their length, her fingers were not strong enough to fulfil her ambition to become a concert pianist.

Shakespeare, the first of her discoveries in literature, was followed by Pope and then Swinburne, a poet frowned upon by her parents' friends and the passion of her adolescence. As a gesture of rebellion and of admiration, Edith ran away for the second time in her life, taking a maid with her and travelling overnight to the Isle of Wight to lay flowers and a libation of milk on Swinburne's grave. This time she came back of her own accord and faced the storms of parental wrath with the stoicism of the disciple.

The garden at Wood End burnt its way into her consciousness. All things were a source of wonder because, she wrote, 'heredity had not yet become a habit'. The summer rain fell 'mauve' over the flowers, the periwinkles were 'innocence' personified. The 'saint blue' skies faded to reveal the gold of the early stars. She was responsive to the patterns of fern and feather mirrored by frost, and of the snowflake reproduced by the crystal, and it was this early consciousness of design that was the basis of the religious faith of her maturity.

She was not, said Osbert Sitwell, a comfortable companion. Her personality was too strong, her mind too imaginative, her heart too easily touched. The bourgeois mentality of conventional young women whose job it was, like that of Mademoiselle Blanchatte in an early prose portrait, to embalm the 'swanlike women whose destiny was the highest society', she rejected, though not without pity. Aware as she was that they were destined to live out their lives rattling 'in the emptiness of other people's splendours', it was these commonplace women who brought her a first glimpse of the evils of poverty. Pity conflicted with rebellion. They were, after all, the jailers of her liberty. Yet, ironically enough, it was a governess who was to become her liberator.

The arrival of Helen Rootham at Renishaw was without a doubt the best thing that could have happened in the life of the lonely, frustrated adolescent who was the young Edith Sitwell. It was a gift for which she was later to pay dearly but the debt took years to accrue and the immediate benefit brooked no gloomy thoughts of future obligations. Helen Rootham, wrote Osbert Sitwell, was 'the first grown-up to appreciate the quality of her young charge'. A cultured, handsome young woman, with a scholar's knowledge of French Symbolist poetry, it was she who introduced Edith Sitwell to one of her few acknowledged influences, the poet Rimbaud. Far from curbing her enthusiasms, she encouraged them. Horizons opened; her pupil made new voyages of discovery without fear either of ridicule or disapproval. Music was a shared experience and Edith, who sat with her back to the races when taken there by her parents, found that she had a companion for other and more enjoyable activities. With Helen Rootham she went to concerts, visited

Edith with her mother

'I was a rather fat little girl: my moon-round face, which was surrounded by green-gold curls had, strangely for so small a child —indeed for any child, the eyes of someone who had witnessed and foretold all the tragedy of the world.' Edith Sitwell, *Taken Care Of*

6

European capitals, saw the works of contemporary painters. Her willingness to appreciate not only the classics but also the work of artists of her day helped to enrich her already heightened sensibilities. She used to say of Debussy that hearing him for the first time was like listening with a squint. Then she became accustomed to his work and Debussy, Ravel and later Stravinsky were the composers who interested her the most.

In 1913, at the age of twenty-five, her freedom was granted her. With Helen Rootham as a chaperone, she was permitted to leave Renishaw for London. Together they shared a flat on the fourth floor of Pembridge Mansions in Bayswater. It was sparsely furnished, with four flights of concrete steps to be climbed before reaching it. There were unaccustomed hardships, cramped quarters, the fire to be lit in the morning, inadequate meals; but they were hardships gladly endured. Pembridge Mansions meant freedom and freedom was all.

After a few weeks of unlikely apprenticeship as a 'ticket of leave' clerk in a government office for which she was paid twenty-five shillings a week, Edith reliquished all thoughts of regular employment and settled down thankfully to write. One of the disadvantages of the Pembridge Mansions flat was that it was too small to house a piano, but this became a secondary consideration, the first being her experiments with poetry.

In 1915 *The Mother*, her first collection of poems, appeared in print. It was a slim volume of ten pages, was privately printed and cost the sum of sixpence to buy. To Edith it was 'the summit of happiness'. She followed it with contributions to *Twentieth Century Harlequinade and Other Poems* published jointly with her brother Osbert. Her major interest was the editing of *Wheels* which appeared at regular intervals from 1916 to 1921. Contributors to *Wheels* were young, some fashionable, all engaged in an act of defiance against the canons of conservative society and the romanticism of the Georgian poets. Not surprisingly, *Wheels* provoked hostility as well as praise. *The New Statesman and Nation* described the editors as 'Harpies like nightingales and nightingales like harpies, chirping balefully upon the walls of old Babylon'. But the 1919 edition had the distinction of publishing six poems by Wilfred Owen and so, for the first of many times, Edith Sitwell was responsible for bringing to

Edith, Osbert and Sacheverell Sitwell. Photograph by Maurice Beck.

'Cyril Connolly: "Were you conscious of being avant garde when you were setting the literary fashion of the twenties?"
Edith Sitwell: "I never thought about it. We were just being ourselves." ' Interview in *The Sunday Times*, 8 September 1957

'Nothing could have been less amateur than my brothers and myself. We were born to be professionals.' Edith Sitwell, *Taken Care Of*

public notice the work of an unknown poet, in this case posthumously, as Wilfred Owen had been killed in action in 1918.

Appreciation of Owen's war poems did not mean that she succumbed to the blandishments of the chauvinists. She set her face against the propaganda which was leading millions to their deaths in the mud-filled trenches of France. 'Nothing will ever make me believe that war is either a good thing or a wise thing, or that there can be any possible justification for sending out some millions of men for the avowed purpose of killing each other', she wrote. War was a 'beastly thing'. More than ever was it necessary to champion the cause of the arts.

The flat at Pembridge Mansions became a centre for literary London. Up the flights of steps toiled the young Aldous Huxley, T. S. Eliot, Virginia Woolf and Harold Acton, joined by notables from other fields such as the actress Mrs. Patrick Campbell, the painter and critic Roger Fry and the photographer Cecil Beaton. With them was the young Chilean who was painting Edith's portrait as the Editor of *Wheels* and with whom she had fallen in love.

This was Alvaro Guevara, darkly handsome, her escort to exhibitions and to concerts and so the man with whom the gossip press linked her name. Guevara was Edith's first real love. It was her misfortune that he was already infatuated with another contributor to *Wheels*, Nancy Cunard, so that, although his feeling for Edith was genuine, she was the object of admiration rather than passion. Perhaps fortunately, he left London for Chile in 1921 and did not return for four years. By that time Edith could accept him as the affectionate friend he remained.

Instead of marriage came fame. By 1920 *Wheels* was in its fifth year. *Clown's House* had appeared and after it *The Wooden Pegasus*. At the age of thirty-two Edith Sitwell was recognized as a poet of stature. It did not make her relationship with Helen Rootham any easier. The 'forceful woman' of contemporary description found it disconcerting to see that her pupil was now something of a celebrity. Already Edith was exchanging letters with Virginia Woolf lamenting the fans who pestered her with missives in need of an answer and complaining about invitations to the 'freak' parties given by the fashionable, those 'smart Bohemians of the little tight hen's heads, giggling and pecking at great reputations'. It was a world from which she recoiled as she had recoiled from the conventions of the middle class.

Success confirmed her philosophy that everyone should be 'burningly anxious to be himself or herself'. 'The aim of flattery', she wrote, 'is to soothe and encourage us by assuring us of the truth of an opinion we have already formed about ourselves.'

It was all the more strongly stated for the insecurity from which it stemmed. As a painfully shy adolescent she had been sent home from her grandmother's house in disgrace because she had conversed at dinner with the elderly Lord Chaplin, at whose head she was being thrown, on the subject of Brahms. Time had subdued but never overcome her shyness, but the fascination she had for photographers and painters convinced her that she had blossomed into a woman of 'a certain gothic elegance'. Acting on the advice of her brother Osbert, she draped her six feet of slender bone structure with brocades decorated by semi-precious jewels so that she looked like a tall tree in flower. Painters were forever asking her to sit for them. For the young photographer Cecil Beaton, introduced to her by Allanah Harper, she became a favourite model. He photographed her in her coffin, *à la* Bernhardt, taking tea in a canopied bed attended by a negress, and walking down the steps at Renishaw flanked by a Borzoi, suitably long-legged and suitably aquiline.

She became known as the High Priestess of poetry and looked the part, wearing a gold turban with fingernails painted to match. Rings weighted the slender fingers. Large brooches were pinned on her brocades, which were worn with bracelets of jet or of amber. But the High Priestess was also a woman who loved to be amused and who chose the music-halls for amusement. Nellie Wallace was a special favourite and, accompanied by Beaton or Guevara or Sacheverell's discovery the young composer William Walton, she would sit in the audience and laugh until the tears rolled down her cheeks.

Happiness she was already defining as 'the inner conviction that one is doing well the thing that one is best fitted to do by nature'. By this definition she was happy, if not fulfilled. No matter how often she asserted that 'artists shouldn't marry', the fact that she was admired rather than desired by the men she loved was a source of unhappiness which she was to admit, not at the time, but in the years to come. In spite of the change in their relationship, Helen Rootham was still a much-needed companion. When her aunt Florence Sitwell gave Edith a present of £3000 she made over a cheque for £1000 to her former governess. Edith's less pleasing discovery that Helen was using the money to help a painter she admired, and that her aunt Florence, incensed at what she thought was the foolish generosity of her niece, had cut her out of her will, did not add to the harmony of the flat in Pembridge Mansions. It may well have been during these years that Edith tasted the first bitterness of disillusion which was to sour the last decade of her life with Helen Rootham. But, she said, 'the greatest possible disadvantage is to be brought up to be polite'. Any open friction was out of the question. Fortunately she was already embarked on a project which was occupying her creative energy. In January

Edith Sitwell in eighteenth-century costume. Photograph by Cecil Beaton.

1922, *Façade*, the 'entertainment' written in collaboration with William Walton, was presented to a privately invited audience at her brother Osbert's house in Carlyle Square. Eighteen months later, in June 1923, the first public performance was given at the Aeolian Hall.

To say that its reception was mixed would be an understatement. 'Never, I think, was a larger and more imposing shower of brickbats hurled at any new work', she wrote, adding that 'these missiles have now been exchanged for equally large and imposing bouquets.' But at the time there was not a bouquet to be seen. Critics, she declared, asked the opinions of a passing postman and the fireman at the hall, and 'These modern substitutes for the Delphic Oracle replied promptly, and in no uncertain terms. They opined that we were mad.'

Façade resulted from 'a kind of dare'. 'Willie gave me certain rhythms and said, "There you are, Edith, see what you can do with that." So I went away and did it. I wanted to prove that I could.'

Her verse was written as a 'work of gaiety' at which 'the audience was meant to laugh'. It was a surrealist experiment in which she was consciously placing assonances and dissonances in deliberate patterns for their effect on rhythm and speed. It reflected the attitude of the post-war poets to the language. The Georgians, they thought, had used a 'tired language' with 'sleepy family habits'. With the peace had come a feeling of rebirth and, she wrote, 'the physical world and its manifestations seemed to us to need re-examination as if we had suddenly burst into life or had gained sight after being blinded from birth.'

New experiments in art are seldom appreciated at once. *Façade* became a connoisseur's piece, hailed only by a few as a masterwork and dismissed by many as incomprehensible. One member of the Aeolian Hall audience was in a position to turn incomprehension to profitable account. This was the young Noël Coward, who promptly included a sketch in his revue *London Calling* featuring 'The Swiss Family Whittlebot' who were, very recognizably, the Sitwells. This was so successful that he followed it with readings over the radio of poems by Miss Hernia Whittlebot. Hernia became a character who appeared regularly in the gossip columns to which Noël Coward would feed titbits of information such as, 'Hernia is busy preparing for the publication of her new book, Gilded Sluts and Garbage. She breakfasts on onions and Vichy water.'

Edith, who enjoyed nothing so much as a literary feud, did not enjoy this debunking by Noël Coward and retired to bed with an attack of jaundice. Both her brothers cut Coward out of their circle of acquaintances, and it was forty years before a reconciliation was brought about.

In the meantime Edith, who admitted that a favourite exercise was to sharpen her claws on the wooden heads of her opponents, returned to the attack. Noël Coward's name appeared more than once in her newspaper articles, accompanied by comments of which this is an example: 'The fierce light that beats upon the throne is nothing to that which shows up Mr. Coward ... [whose] elephantine wit lumbers and scampers breathlessly after an emotion as frail and destructive as a clothes moth.'

From which it will be seen that she was well able to fight her own battles. Being a controversial figure, these were many. Dr. F. R. Leavis, University Reader in English at Cambridge University, made the public observation that 'the Sitwells belonged to the history of publicity', thus earning the Sitwell animosity. Edith sharpened her claws and noted that, 'The Doctor has a transcendental gift, when he is writing sense, for making this appear to be nonsense.' It was, she said, 'sad to see Milton's great lines bobbing up and down in the sandy desert of Dr. Leavis's mind with the grace of a fleet of weary camels.' Geoffrey Grigson, co-editor of what she described as 'a paper called New Verse of inordinate and notorious funniness', and Wyndham Lewis were two favourite targets. One scathing chapter of her *Aspects of Modern Poetry*, which appeared in 1934, was devoted to them. She admitted in a letter to Christabel Aberconway that she had laughed until she 'nearly cried' as she was writing it, but her critics did not all enjoy the joke. G. W. Stonier, reviewing her book for *The New Statesman and Nation*, accused her of plagiarism, both from Leavis and Grigson, and one of the many Sitwell controversies was waged in the correspondence columns of the paper.

As the years went on her fame grew, and the publication of *Bucolic Comedies* (1923), *The Sleeping Beauty* (1924), *Troy Park* (1925), *Elegy on Dead Fashion* (1926), *Rustic Elegies* (1927), *Five Poems* (1928) and *Gold Coast Customs* (1929) all confirmed her place as the High Priestess of English poetry. So assiduous were her devotees that she escaped from them across the channel. It was in 1923 that the first of her annual visits to Paris took place, her refuge being a flat in the rue Saint-Dominique belonging to Madame Evelyn Wiel, younger sister of Helen Rootham. Escape gave her freedom to work but not the peace she was seeking. It was not very long after she had settled in at the rue Saint-Dominique that she met the second love of her life, the painter Pavel Tchelitchew.

When they met she was already thirty-eight. 'A hieratic figure in Limoges enamel,' wrote Harold Acton, 'the pale oval face with its almond eyes and long thin nose had often been carved in ivory by true believers. Her entire figure possessed a distinction seldom to be seen outside the glass cases of certain museums.'

Edith Sitwell
Pencil drawing by Wyndham Lewis. 1921. National Portrait Gallery, London.

EDITH SITWELL

Wyndham Lewis
1921

Like so many painters before him Tchelitchew was fascinated by what he saw. She remembered him circling around her at a première 'clapping his large painter's hands' as he did so. They were introduced by Gertrude Stein, the patron who had 'burgled' his studio during his absence and bought everything she had taken.

'I have an Englishwoman for Pavlik to paint,' she said to Stella Bowen. Stella Bowen, mistress of the novelist Ford Madox Ford and a painter in her own right, was a mutual friend who knew Tchelitchew too well to be entirely happy about the introduction. Stein herself prefaced their meeting with a warning: 'If I present Pavlik to you,' she said to Edith, 'it is your responsibility. His character is not my affair.' Her warning delivered, she invited them both to one of her weekly soirées held in the rue de Fleurus in the studio lined with the work of Picasso, Matisse, Juan Gris and Tchelitchew. Here Gertrude Stein held court to the writers, painters and musicians of her day, enthroned in an armchair in which, wrote Allanah Harper, 'she looked like a mixture of a Roman Emperor and an early Buddhist sculpture.' Whether her motive was to provide Tchelitchew with a patron or to present Edith with a painter who would do justice to her appearance, history does not relate. What Stein had not bargained on was that Edith would fall in love.

When they met, Tchelitchew was living in 'a little black hole of an apartment in the Boulevard Montparnasse' but it was not much later that he moved into a cottage in which Stella Bowen had been living with Ford Madox Ford, in Guermantes, a tiny hamlet thirty-eight kilometres from Paris. It was complete with garden and orchard, the rent was nominal and, in spite of his uncertain income, he was able to invite his sister Choura and his friend, the pianist Allen Tanner, to live with him.

All Paris knew that Tchelitchew and Allen Tanner were lovers but Edith never seemed to have been aware of their relationship. Protected by her upbringing and by the fact that she herself was sharing her accommodation with another woman, she accepted Allen Tanner in Tchelitchew's life as she accepted Helen Rootham in her own. Friends such as Stella Bowen and Allanah Harper saw what was happening and deplored it. But to inform Edith Sitwell that she had fallen in love with a homosexual would have been a formidable task. Unhappiness was the inevitable result but, as the years went on, friendship developed and with it a degree of fulfilment for both. For the first time in her life Edith dared to go on holiday with a man. Their correspondence, written in English or French and usually in a mixture of both, shows an aesthetic, if not a physical affinity. They quarrelled. Tchelitchew, typically Russian in temperament, insisted that he be the dominant one of their relationship. 'Ôtez les pantalons!' he stormed at her. Edith, outraged, demanded that he explain himself, which he did, in English. 'Kindly leave the trousers to me. You must stop being Joan of Arc. The rôle doesn't suit you and you'll only be beaten. Two people cannot rule.'

Edith, essentially feminine by nature, no doubt rather enjoyed the domination. Meanwhile Tchelitchew painted her obsessively; in mauve with her 'green gold hair' shoulder length and 'the most beautiful nose any woman ever had' well in evidence; in red with a turban on her head; seated, pen in hand, looking every inch the poet. The result was six portraits and a head in wax, thought by many to be the most imaginative of all. That she had a fascination for him is obvious. Parker Tyler in his biography states that Tchelitchew found in Edith's 'beautiful sheltered eroticism, the purely passive female sensibility that lives forever'. The American poet William Carlos Williams quoted Tchelitchew's description of her as, 'A very beautiful woman. She is alone. She is very positive and very emotional. She takes herself very seriously and seems to be as cold as ice. She is not so.'

Edith, denied fulfilment, found an outlet in her rôle of patron to his work. She arranged a *vernissage* in Paris, another in London. In *The Graphic* of 28 July 1928 she stated that 'the day on which I first began to realize Tchelitchew's pictures was one of the most important days in my artistic life.'

'Artists should not marry', she repeated. It was a comforting philosophy from which she drew much-needed strength. This was the period of her life which she looked back upon as 'unmitigated hell'. A good part of the reason was that these were her years of involvement. The poet who said of herself that she had always been 'a little outside life' was now faced with reality at its sternest. In 1930 Helen Rootham discovered the cancer which, eight years later, was to end her life. Edith, with only a small private income at her disposal, was forced to turn to prose to supplement it. The liberator who had brought her freedom had become a dependent needing her support. She turned to biography and to journalism. Two 'lives', of Alexander Pope and of Victoria of England, were interspersed with *English Eccentrics* and her history of Bath. She became a regular contributor to *The Sunday Referee*, and her articles appeared in dailies such as *The Evening Standard* and *The Yorkshire Evening Post*. They were controversial, usually written as a challenge to the values of her day, often witty and always widely read. None the less, it was not until she was working on her last work of prose, her novel based on the life of Swift, *I Live Under a Black Sun*, that she felt satisfied. It was, she told her friend Rée Gorer, 'the only prose book of mine (excepting for criticism) that I've ever

Edith Sitwell
Charcoal drawing by Albert Rutherston. 1928. Humanities Research Center, University of Texas, Austin.

14

been pleased with'. She wrote it in the early hours of the morning, starting work at 5.30 or 6.00 at the latest, this being 'the only time when I can be sure of quiet'.

Poetry seemed to have become a thing of the past. Although she defined it as 'the deification of reality', in her case at least, it demanded perspective. Caught up in the illness of a friend, in the practical work associated with it, and struggling with her unfulfilled passion for Tchelitchew in these the difficult middle years of her life, she was enmeshed by the immediate. The long sight of the poet was focused, perforce, on the minutiae of daily living. It was not until she was able to detach herself again that the gift of poetry was restored to her.

Helen Rootham's death, though in every sense a release, was a personal blow. Another was Tchelitchew's departure for America. Osbert, worried about the world war that was looming so ominously on the horizon, persuaded her to come back to live in England. Her parents were no longer at Renishaw and so Edith could live there as his guest. Sorrowing over the beloved cat she was forced to leave behind in Paris, she arranged for a small income to be paid to Evelyn Wiel, now divorced and so able to return to her flat at the rue Saint-Dominique. Neither of the Roothams were ever hesitant about accepting the money offered them by Edith. The tiny income enabled Evelyn to remain in Paris. It is to her everlasting credit that she not only survived the occupation but managed to retain Edith's cat, her collection of paintings by Tchelitchew, her books, and, sealed up in a wall cupboard, her manuscripts.

With the publication of *Street Songs* in 1942, Edith was acclaimed once more as a major poet. Macmillan, now established as her publishers, brought out her *Poet's Notebook*. In 1944 her second collection appeared under the title *Green Song* and in the last year of the war came *The Song of the Cold*, a new anthology of her work. It was a second flowering, considered by most critics to be her best. Praise poured in from Richard Church, G. S. Fraser, Cyril Connolly and Kenneth Clark. Free of the pressures of the immediate, the long sight of the poet was restored. The 'deep humanist passion' recognized by the critic Jack Lindsay replaced the personal frustrations of the last decade. Her style had changed. She used long lines, very often unrhymed, with 'assonances and half assonances used outwardly and inwardly in the lines, to act as ground rhythm.' She wrote about 'the world reduced to the Ape as mother, teacher, protector', and she wrote about the faith which redeemed it. 'Now,' wrote John Russell in the *Sunday Times*, 'she belongs to the greatest tradition of English religious poetry.'

In her own eyes she was a working woman. She liked to go to bed early. Her day began in the early hours. It was a discipline made possible by the leisurely way of life at Renishaw now that Osbert Sitwell was in residence. 'Nobody comes down to breakfast', she wrote to T. S. Eliot. 'People disappear for hours on end if they want to . . . nobody is ever harried or badgered.'

Inspiration reached apotheosis with *The Shadow of Cain*, regarded by some critics, and more particularly Jack Lindsay, as a masterpiece. Lindsay's understanding of her work brought her a rare satisfaction. He seemed, she said, 'to have lived through all the processes of my poetry.' His review brought new incentive as did the flattering interest taken in her work by contemporary composers. Benjamin Britten wrote a deeply moving setting for her war poem 'Still Falls the Rain'. Humphrey Searle, who had already written a score for *Gold Coast Customs*, now suggested that he present a setting of *The Shadow of Cain* at the Palace Theatre with Edith and her latest poetic discovery, Dylan Thomas, as readers.

The Shadow of Cain appeared in 1947, the year of Edith's sixtieth birthday. She was an honorary doctor of literature, a unique personality, a poet with a body of work behind her. In their separate ways her brothers had also achieved eminence. It was inevitable that, sooner or later, the Sitwells would receive invitations from the United States which were irresistible enough to lure them across the Atlantic. On 11 December 1948 Bennett Cerf recorded the party given in their honour for the benefit of *The Saturday Review*. The guest list included W. H. Auden, Tennessee Williams, Carson McCullers, Marianne Moore and Stephen Spender, all being mobbed like movie stars by the crowds invited in their honour.

At this time Edith's *bête noire* was D. H. Lawrence, mainly because Renishaw was so obviously the setting that he had used for his *Lady Chatterley's Lover*. News of the feud had evidently crossed the Atlantic and Cerf uses this as his introduction:

' "I hear you were very funny once in Liverpool," I shouted above the din . . . Dr. Edith beamed . . . and said, "Sit down here with me. The incident to which you refer occurred when I was discussing the poetry of D. H. Lawrence. I said it was 'soft, woolly, and hot like a Jaeger sweater.' I thought Lawrence would have a fit but he didn't. The Jaegers, however, did. They informed me indignantly that their sweaters were indeed soft and woolly, but never hot, due to their special system of slow conductivity." '

Cerf's account gives a glimpse of 'Dr. Edith's' transatlantic popularity. It was the first of many such invitations, including one from Hollywood to write a film script for her *Fanfare for Elizabeth*, first published in 1946.

Edith set sail, this time for the West, booked into a hotel in Los Angeles, re-established contact with her old friend Aldous Huxley and gave audience to Hollywood's notables. This, she reported, led to 'a Laocoön entanglement' with Mary Pickford and a

Edith Sitwell with Sir William and Lady Walton at the Royal
Society of Literature garden party in July 1953.

'royal encounter' with the Queen of Hollywood, Ethel
Barrymore, which was 'delightful, although Osbert
ascribes my bronchitis to her, as she was breathing
heavily.'

In due course the work on the script was completed
in spite of a collaborator whose approach she
memorized for the benefit of her friends. 'In this scene
you have those Cardinal guys threatening the King
with everlasting damnation. And the King says:
"That's O.K. by me, boys! Go right ahead. You tell
your boss the Pope that I am King of England—and to
hell with his everlasting damnation!"'

Not surprisingly, the film never materialized. There
were flickerings of interest reported by George Cukor,
especially from Vivien Leigh who, he said, was 'in love
with the script'. But apathy prevailed and *Fanfare for
Elizabeth* swelled the archives of abandoned film
scripts. With the money she had been paid, Edith
bought two large aquamarines, referred to thereafter as
her 'wages of sin', and sailed for home. A new honour

awaited her in 1954, when she was made a Dame of the
British Empire. To her honorary doctorates she could
now add the final accolade. Dame Edith Sitwell made
the pleasing, if disconcerting, discovery that she had
become a national institution.

If the first decade of her life was the most painful,
this last part was the most glorious. Her dress and the
frankness of her public utterances ensured her popularity with the press. Statements were seized upon and
quoted like oracles from the sibyl.

'All women should have a day a week in bed', and
'English women who will dress as though they had
been a mouse in a previous incarnation', are two
examples. The majority hailed her as part of the
tradition of eccentricity which she herself had hal-
lowed. To the minority she was England's major
woman poet. The publication of her *Collected Poems*
elicited from Cyril Connolly comparison with Yeats
and Auden: 'her [poems] have the purest intention of
any', he wrote, 'the honey may sometimes fail, but it is
never adulterated.' Kenneth Clark claimed that 'those
who care for poetry recognized a true poetic and

prophetic cry which had not been heard in English since the death of Yeats.' Throughout her writing-life, controversy had raged about her far from hapless head. This last decade proved to be no exception. Those who delighted in her eccentricity disapproved of her poetry. Those who delighted in her poetry disapproved of her eccentricity.

Fame brought her gratification but happiness continued to elude her. The death of Dylan Thomas, that 'poor, dear and most wonderful poet' whose work she had first brought to the notice of the public, was followed by the news that her beloved brother Osbert had been stricken with Parkinson's disease. Edith turned to the Roman Catholic Church. Her religious sense had been deepening over the years and her conversion was genuine if unorthodox. She was in need of support. As the years went by her anxieties intensified. Between Osbert Sitwell and herself lay the shadow, not only of his illness, but of her dependence upon him. Her overdraft was mounting to frightening proportions. She suffered from her rôle of poor relation but there was no alternative open to her. It was as her brother's guest that she spent her summers in Renishaw and her winters in Montegufoni, Osbert's Italian residence. Only for a few short weeks in spring and autumn did she achieve independence. These were her seasons in London, when she lived at the Sesame Club in Grosvenor Street.

It was to the Sesame Club that I made my way when, in the autumn of 1957, I became her secretary.

We had actually met a few months before at the Aldeburgh Festival where she was reciting Blake with C. Day Lewis at the invitation of Benjamin Britten. It was a day of high summer and her appearance was as gothic as her legend demanded. Over an ankle length black satin dress she wore a Chinese coat of gold flecked with green. Her Tudor hat was studded with gold and framed by two lengths of black chiffon. Three aquamarines of enormous size caught the light slanting through the stained glass windows of the parish church. To complete the picture she wore dark glasses with mirror rims that slanted diabolically towards the temples and protected her from the sun. As a façade it was awe-inspiring, but I was to discover that the woman behind the façade was a very human being. The scars of childhood had left her vulnerable. Though conscious of her public persona and insisting upon its recognition—a favourite adjective applied to the irreverent was 'impertinent'—the grandeur of the presentation was a deliberate protection behind which the kindly, generous, essentially unsophisticated person she was could shelter.

Her wit was still used as a weapon. The wooden heads of her opponents continued to feel her claws, but malice was reserved for her enemies. To those who served her she was unfailingly courteous. As aristocrat and artist her contempt for the hierarchy of class was ingrained. A parlour maid was listened to with the respect she showed a duchess. Towards the importunates who revealed their lack of talent, towards her literary antagonists, and towards those who failed in respect, she was merciless. After a reading of her poetry at the Festival Hall, London, an event for which every seat had been sold for weeks beforehand, a club member confided that she had been unable to attend her 'little concert'. 'We *all* missed you', Edith replied sweetly.

Among those country people who used the Sesame Club for their week-end visits she was an exotic apparition. The word 'exhibitionist' hissed through their midst. Those who tried to crash her acquaintance smarted from the snubs they received. Those for whom the conventions were the law frowned on her as a deserter from their ranks. The staff, in the meantime, continued to serve her with devotion and to regard her as the uncrowned queen of the club, an attitude shared by her chauffeur, a portly gentleman of immense respectability and the unlikely name of Raper, who drove her in a hired Daimler of mammoth proportions.

This then was Edith Sitwell at sixty-nine, a vital, formidable personage whose invitations were accepted by the great on both sides of the Atlantic. To the Sesame Club came writers such as C. P. Snow and his wife Pamela Hansford-Johnson, Stephen Spender, Gore Vidal, Graham Greene and Henry Cecil; critics such as Cyril Connolly; composers such as Benjamin Britten and Humphrey Searle; actors such as Alec Guinness and Sir John Gielgud; old friends like John Lehmann, Sir Kenneth and Lady Clark and Cecil Beaton, Mr. and Mrs. John Hay Whitney and Carson McCullers. The list was endless. In spite of her overdraft, her entertaining was both lavish and intensive. There were usually two parties a day, luncheon followed by drinks at 5.30. This she kept up for the duration of her London visits, maintaining a nucleus of young people who were the constants among her guests: the poet Alberto de Lacerda, the pianist Gordon Watson, the publisher Michael Stapleton, and myself. Young people were a stimulus to her and, at Quentin Stevenson's suggestion, she had no hesitation in inviting the 'beat' poets, Allen Ginsberg and Gregory Corso, to lunch.

It was an incongruous gathering, although not quite as bizarre as the account which appeared later in *Life* magazine. According to this, the conversation was devoted to the use of marijuana cigarettes, the menu consisting of watercress sandwiches and tea. In fact it was a meal that had been especially ordered, beginning with smoked salmon and lobster thermidor and ending with the club's speciality, an ice-cream *bombe à l'américaine*.

The subject of drug-taking arose from a discussion about Aldous Huxley's experiments with mescalin. All three young poets admitted to the general use of

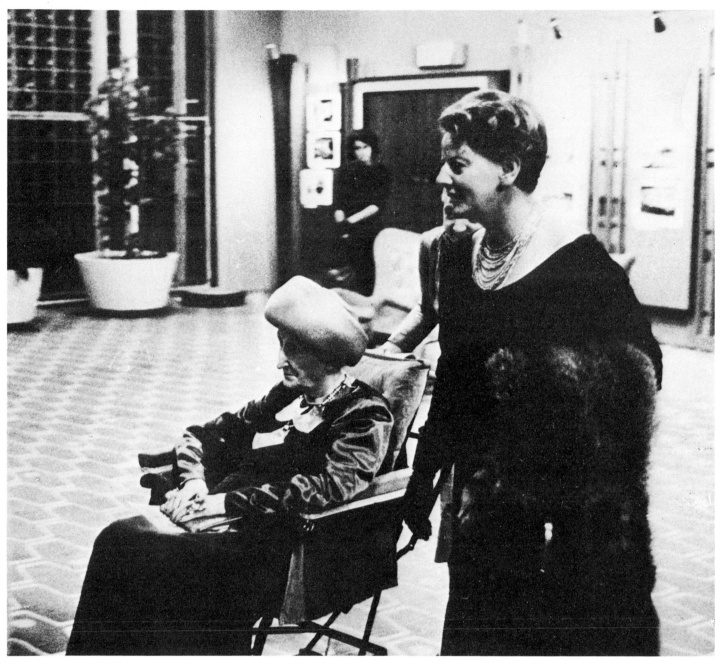

Edith Sitwell being wheeled through the foyer of the Royal Festival Hall, London, on her way to recite her later poetry at her 'Memorial Concert', as she called it. Pushing the wheelchair is her nurse Sister Farquhar and on the right Elizabeth Salter.

marijuana amongst their contemporaries and defended it on the grounds of 'heightened sensibility'. Edith's answer, in no sense a judgement, was simply that 'no poet should need a drug to produce extreme sensibility, which must be, if he is any good, a part of his equipment.'

At this point she was not, as reported, offered a marijuana cigarette, refused on the grounds that marijuana brought her out in spots. It would have taken a great deal more courage than any of the three young men possessed to have offered Edith Sitwell a 'reefer'. Characteristically, when she read this account to me later on, it was not the imputation that she smoked marijuana that upset her as much as the doubts cast on her complexion.

'I am hardly the spot queen', she complained.

To the faithful she remained the High Priestess of English poetry and for the Edinburgh Festival of 1959 came an invitation that she give a reading of her poetry at the Lyceum Theatre. This turned out to be a source of more unwanted publicity and for the reason that she refused then, as she had refused all her life, to defer to public opinion.

When the curtain went up she was seated centre stage, resplendent in purple and gold. Her cloak fell behind her like a train and around her neck was the gold collar which had been commissioned for her by an American millionairess known as 'Bryher', but which looked Aztec enough to arouse the interest of the British Museum. It was an appreciative audience and her appearance was greeted by applause. This she acknowledged, then put on her glasses, picked up her typescript and began.

Unfortunately, some members of her audience were

not as punctual as she was. Latecomers poured in. The inevitable rustle of chocolate boxes and programmes was interspersed with whispered apologies. A voice shouted from the auditorium: 'We can't hear!'

At first Edith took no notice. She had once told me that when she and Dylan Thomas were reciting in America there were always two deaf old ladies seated somewhere in the audience who complained because they could not hear. This was so regular that Dylan used to ask her before the performance where the afflicted pair would be found that night. Now she read on, her beautiful voice pitched on the level decided upon at the rehearsal.

Other voices informed her that they, too, could not hear. Edith lowered her typescript and snapped at them:

'In that case pay more attention.'

'But we can't hear you.'

'Then get a hearing aid.'

There was a shocked silence. Round one had been won. Edith adjusted her glasses and began to read once more.

It seemed that the audience had not yet learned its lesson. Perhaps they enjoyed the unusual experience of provoking an artist, normally separated from them by the barrier of the footlights.

'We still can't hear', they shouted.

This was heresy indeed. Edith lowered her typescript and removed her glasses.

'I have earned my living by reciting across America and if you can't hear me there is something wrong with you. I have no intention of ruining my voice to please you.'

She then picked up her typescript for the third time. A courageous member of the dress circle decided that here lay the explanation of the difficulty.

'If you lower your papers it would be better. Then we could see your face', he suggested.

'You won't like it if you do see it', Edith informed him.

I don't quite know what I expected to happen then—perhaps a riot of angry people demanding their money back. Panicking badly, I hurried backstage to instruct them to lower the curtain.

Fortunately by the time I arrived backstage the audience had admitted defeat. They had also learned an important lesson. Not a sound came from anywhere in the auditorium. They paid her the compliment she had expected in the first place. They listened.

The newspapers had a field day. Every reporter in the building rushed to the telephone to wire the news to the evening papers. On the following day it received world coverage. What they did not report was the postscript to the story.

After the performance Edith remained in her dressing-room, chatting with Graham Greene, Lord Harewood and Sir Compton Mackenzie, who had come round to see her. It was almost an hour later before she drove back to her hotel, yet waiting outside the stage door was a crowd of between 300 and 500 people. They pressed around the car, close enough for me to see the expression on their faces. It was by no means just curiosity. They beamed affection and admiration, cheering her as she drove off. 'The Scots always like a fighter' was her comment.

Edinburgh was only one of her many public appearances. She went to Oxford to give what was to be the last of her readings of *Façade*. She was one of the panel on 'The Brains Trust'. She visited schools, lectured at the Royal Society of Literature, gave the address at Charles Morgan's memorial service and appeared opposite John Freeman, later British Ambassador to the United States, on Hugh Burnett's controversial television series *Face to Face*. Since she never refused a challenge, she accepted her commitments, exhausting though they sometimes were and protesting as she did so that she was a 'working woman' who was never allowed to get on with her work.

Her output continued to be impressive. Macmillan's publication of her *Collected Poems* was followed by *The Atlantic Book of British and American Poetry*, which she edited for Little, Brown in America. Then, after a selection from Swinburne for the London publisher Victor Gollancz, came the second of her books on Elizabeth I, *The Queens and the Hive*. Finally Macmillan brought out a slim volume of her later poetry written in the face of illness and including some of the best of her shorter lyrical poems. For one, 'La Bella Bona Roba' she received the Guinness Award. Another was 'Prothalamium' written for the wedding of the Duke of Kent. Her so-called autobiography *Taken Care Of*, put together as a last gesture of failing vitality, was published posthumously.

Her *Queens and the Hive* was the means of reconciliation with her former 'debunker', Noël Coward. It had been dedicated to George Cukor, their mutual friend, and it was he who suggested that they meet. Edith issued an invitation to tea and in due course, Sir Noël appeared. By this time Edith had moved into a flat in Hampstead and they sat opposite each other in her small sitting-room, Sir Noël wearing dark glasses because of a complaint that he described, cheerfully, as 'pink-eye', Edith in her latest hat, her inevitable fur coat and slippers. Sir Noël sipped his tea and refused sandwiches. Edith went through the motions of lifting her cup to her lips and putting it down untouched.

Sir Noël set the ball rolling by apologizing for having hurt her feelings, pleading youth. Edith accepted his apology with a warmth that proved past

Edith Sitwell, 1962. Photograph by Mark Gerson.

Edith Sitwell complained that the photograph 'made a pet of all my wrinkles'.

resentments had not only been banished but forgotten. They then went on to discuss 'Willie' (Somerset) Maugham and his legal battle with his daughter. They were on different sides of this notorious controversy, Coward explained that he was very fond of Maugham's wife. Edith confessed to a dislike of the lady. She admitted though that she found Maugham something of a strain. In fact, she had once tried to avoid meeting him at the London bookshop Bumpus by picking up an imaginary book under a table.

'Poor Willie,' she said, 'he simply followed me under the table so that we encountered each other on all fours. "E-e-edith," he said to me, "wh-what are you doing down here?"'

It was the discovery of a shared enemy that brought them into triumphant accord. Edith nursed a grievance against the American columnist Dorothy Kilgallin, who had corrected her punctuation in each of the syndicated newspapers for which she wrote. Sir Noël, it transpired, had a similar aversion to the lady.

'Do tell me,' Edith asked him, 'what is she like?'

Sir Noël's reply was instantaneous. 'My dear Dame Edith, she is one brisk stampede from nose to navel.'

By the time he left they were both regretting the feud which had kept them apart. As I helped Sir Noël into his coat, I told him that I felt I had been present at an historic occasion. Sir Noël did not indulge in false modesty. 'You have been', he agreed genially.

Coward's visit was followed by the last great occasion of her life. This was her 'memorial concert', as she insisted upon calling it, arranged as a celebration of her seventy-fifth birthday. The programme was to start with Edith reading some of her later poetry. *Still Falls the Rain* was to be performed by Benjamin Britten and Peter Pears and *Façade* was to be conducted by Sir William Walton. In the Royal Box were the members of her family, Sir Osbert, very frail and stooped because of the illness which was by now advanced; Sacheverell, tall, fresh-faced, his triangular smile so like hers; his wife Georgia, his son Reresby and Penelope, Reresby's wife; Edith's nurse and myself. Francis, Sacheverell's younger son, was to guide her wheelchair onto the platform. By 1962 Edith's health had failed her. Only her sense of occasion empowered her to meet this, the last great public challenge that she was to face.

The concert was preceded by an onslaught of dressmakers, hat-makers, manicurists and beauty parlour experts. For her dress she decided on red velvet, as that had been the material chosen for her by Tchelitchew when she had given a recital in Paris more than thirty years before. It had long satin sleeves of the same colour, and a high, round neck in order to show off the gold collar that she always wore on state occasions. Her hat, modelled on a becoming black straw with a wide turned-back brim that she already possessed, was also gold, as were the shoes below the folds of her skirt. An appointment was made for a 'facial' to be given by an expert a few hours before the event. For public appearances her face was made up with an attention to detail that would have done justice to a film star. Green was chosen for eye-shadow, a colour that effectively accentuated the hooded depth of her eyes. Her lipstick matched the red of her nails. Proud of the fact that it was she who had set the fashion for gold and silver nail-polish in the 1920s, she sometimes experimented by gilding her nails, but for the concert she decided on red as the colour that, at this stage of her life, showed off her hands to the best advantage.

The Festival Hall was packed. Some were invited guests, most came for what was generally understood to be the last appearance of a charismatic personality. Full use was made of the drama of the occasion.

A spotlight caught the scarlet figure in the wheelchair, turned to face the audience. Behind her Francis Sitwell stood in attendance. Edith rustled her typescript and adjusted her glasses. The businesslike way she put on these utilitarian objects created its own contrast. It was as though the intellectual was bidding us forget the illusion created by the great eccentric. 'The effect has been achieved, now we must concentrate on the matter in hand', she seemed to be saying, while the glasses, perched insecurely on the elegant nose, pushed up the brim of her hat.

Her voice was deeper, more slurred, rather softer than of old, but on this night there was nobody to say they could not hear.

The silence in the auditorium conveyed much more than just the quality of listening. It was the hush of respect. The grand old lady who made a throne out of her wheel-chair and intoned her opulent images was crowned that night by her achievements. She read the poem born of the quotation from St. Agnes, 'His Blood Colours My Cheek', the tiny lyric that was the fruit of her old age, 'A Girl's Song in Winter', 'Choric Song' and 'Prothalamium'. All but two of the poems had been written since her seventieth birthday. 'Still Falls the Rain' was followed by *Façade*, read by Irene Worth and Sebastian Shaw.

As audience to her own work for the first time in her life, Edith did not entirely approve of the performance that night. But the critic who was later to quote her words on the subject should have remembered that it was the performer and not the creator of *Façade* who criticized it. As performer, she had a possessive prejudice towards a rôle that she regarded as her own. As creator, she was aware of the tribute being paid to her and responded, joining in the tumultuous applause that followed.

The speakers came back to take their applause. They returned with Sir William Walton, and the applause continued. We waited for the moment when the performers would turn towards the Royal Box, but before this could happen the audience decided to pay its own tribute. The entire 3000 wheeled round to face her. Looking down, the movement of upraised hands was like a current in a sea swirling in her direction. They clapped, they cheered, they stampeded. Edith made an effort to rise out of her wheel-chair in an acknowledgement, but could not. Instead she lifted her hands and waved back, crying without self-consciousness.

Of all the rapturous press reports, her favourite was a piece from the *Daily Sketch*. She telephoned the next morning in order to read it to me.

'My dear, you must listen to this. Some nice young man that I never met was evidently holding my hand as I went off to sleep. This is what he says about me: "A wonderful, exasperating, intelligent woman, before she pulled up the sheets and slipped into sleep, she said, 'Be kind to me. Like the poet Yeats said, "I have spread my dreams under your feet. Tread softly because you tread on my dreams."'" According to him, I uttered these famous last words: "'Don't trample on me because so many people do.' And then our greatest woman poet fell asleep." Goodness!'

Her last eighteen months were a battle against failing health. She fought it with wit and the courage that was integral to her character. Peace of mind had been restored by sales of her manuscripts and her collection of Tchelitchews. These had established a comfortable bank balance and so procured her independence. My final discovery of the cache of paintings and manuscripts in the wall-papered cupboard of her Paris flat encouraged her to obey the advice of her doctors and embark on a sea voyage to escape the English winter. At the age of seventy-six, with Sister Farquhar her nurse and myself as her companions, Edith Sitwell set sail around the world. But courage was betrayed by the elements. At Bermuda she was taken off the ship on a stretcher and flown back to London. A move to a tiny Georgian cottage opposite Keats's house in Hampstead brought her a few months of peace. Friends and family made the pilgrimage to Bryher Cottage, as she had called it after her American supporter and friend, as they had done to the Sesame Club. She worked, as she had worked all her life, putting the finishing touches to her autobiography, selecting passages for a prose selection she was planning. On the night before her death, she was giving her final approval to the photographs for her autobiography.

Edith Sitwell died, three months after her seventy-seventh birthday, on 9 December 1964. Obituaries the world over marked the event. The longest and most appreciative appeared in London's *The Times* which declared that her death had left contemporary English poetry the poorer, continuing with an analysis of her work which could not be bettered:

'Her poetry was not in the Arnoldian sense a criticism of life but was a poetry essentially of praise and transformation. She combined a taste for elaborate and latterly for sweeping technical effects with a basic simplicity of vision: a vision deeply affected in her early poems by childhood memories, and in her later poems by a mixture of deep horror at the violence and cruelty of the world with profound faith in the ultimate goodness of God and holiness of nature.' (*The Times*, 10 December 1964).

Edith Sitwell had asked of herself, 'To what ideals would I reach in my poetry?'

'To produce a poetry that is the light of the Great Morning wherein all beings whom we see passing in the common street are transformed into the epitome of all beauty, or of all joy, or of all sorrow.'

'My poems are hymns of praise to the glory of Life.'

CHRONOLOGY OF PUBLICATIONS

1915   *The Mother*

1916   *Twentieth Century Harlequinade* (a joint volume of poetry with Osbert Sitwell)
Wheels, First Cycle

1917   *Wheel, Second Cycle*

1918   *Clowns' Horses*
Wheels, Third Cycle

1919   *Wheels, Fourth Cycle*

1920   *The Wooden Pegasus*
Children's Tales from the 1920 Russian Ballet
Wheels, Fifth Cycle

1921   *Wheels, Sixth Cycle*

1922   *Façade*

1923   *Bucolic Comedies*

1924   *The Sleeping Beauty*

1925   *Troy Park*
Poetry and Criticism
Poor Young People (a joint volume of poetry with Osbert and Sacheverell Sitwell)

1926   *Elegy on Dead Fashion*
Augustan Books of Modern Poetry
Poem for a Christmas Card

1927   *Rustic Elegies*

1928   *Popular Song*
Five Poems

1929   *Gold Coast Customs*

1930   *Alexander Pope*
Collected Poems

1931   *In Spring*
Jane Barston
Epithalamium

1932   *Bath* (a history of Bath)

1933   *English Eccentrics* (a volume of essays)
Five Variations on a Theme

1934   *Aspects of Modern Poetry* (a volume of criticism)

1936   *Victoria of England*
Selected Poems

1937   *I Live under a Black Sun* (a novel based on the life of Jonathan Swift)

1938   *Trio* (a volume of essays by Edith, Osbert and Sacheverell Sitwell)

1940   *Poems New and Old*

1942   *Street Songs*
English Women

1943   *A Poet's Notebook* (a volume of essays)

1944   *Green Song*

1945   *The Weeping Babe*
The Song of the Cold (an anthology)

1946   *Fanfare for Elizabeth* (a biography of Elizabeth I)

1947   *The Shadow of Cain*

1948   *A Notebook on William Shakespeare*

1949   *The Canticle of the Rose*

1950   *Poor Men's Music*
Façade and Other Poems

1952   *Selected Poems*

1953   *Gardeners and Astronomers*
The Pocket Poets

1954   *Collected Poems* (first published in the United States in 1954 and in Great Britain in 1957)

1962   *The Outcasts*
The Queens and the Hive (a study of Elizabeth I and Mary, Queen of Scots)

1965   *Taken Care Of* (an autobiography, published posthumously)

FAMILY AND HOME

Thus spake the lady underneath the trees:
I was a member of a family
Whose legend was of hunting—(all the rare
And unattainable brightness of the air)—
A race whose fabled skill in falconry
Was used on the small songbirds and a winged
And blinded Destiny . . .

Edith Sitwell, 'Colonel Fantock'

Lady Ida Sitwell
Oil Painting by Sir William Richmond. Collection of Reresby Sitwell.

'My mother was very beautiful, with a face that, in youth, had the pomp and magnificence of a Roman mask. In old age the mask was still magnificent and its pride was unbowed but it was empty. She considered that she had married beneath her and, in moments of anger would hurl at me: "*I* am better born than you".' Edith Sitwell to the author

Lady Ida in middle age

Sir George Sitwell, c. 1885

My father had 'much of the physical splendour of a fourteenth-century Italian noble. His dignity of bearing... his rather strange pale eyes, all added to that effect.' Elizabeth Salter, *The Last Years of a Rebel*
'Apart from the fact that he had married my mother [his] principal worry was that the world did not understand that it had been created in order to prove his theories.'   Edith Sitwell, *Taken Care Of*

Sir George Sitwell at Montegufoni

'In 1909 Sir George bought the vast Castle of Montegufoni in the hills of Tuscany... and spent the next thirty years restoring and refurnishing the Castle *as it might have been* in the days of its former owners, the Acciaiuoli, Florentine bankers and Dukes of Athens in the Middle Ages.'   Reresby Sitwell, *Renishaw Hall and the Sitwells*

27

Montegufoni, c. 1920

Sir George announced the news to his family in a letter to Osbert, then a schoolboy of sixteen.

'You will be interested to hear that I am buying in your name the Castle of Acciaiuoli . . . there is a great tower, a picture gallery with frescoed portraits of the owners from a very early period, and a chapel full of relics of the Saints. There are the remains of a charming old terraced garden, not very large, with two or three statues, a pebblework grotto and rows of flower pots with the family arms upon them. The great saloon, now divided into several rooms, opens into an interior court where one can take one's meals in hot weather . . . We shall be able to grow our own fruit, wine, oil—even champagne!'   Osbert Sitwell, *Left Hand, Right Hand!*

Sir George and Lady Ida at Scarborough, c. 1934

In the 1920s Sir George and Lady Ida settled permanently at Montegufoni but they 'came over most years to visit their sons and the whole family would foregather at Renishaw'.   Reresby Sitwell, *Renishaw Hall and the Sitwells*

28

But Dagobert and Peregrine and I
Were children then; we walked like shy gazelles
Among the music of the thin flower-bells.
And life still held some promise,—never ask
Of what —

Edith Sitwell, 'Colonel Fantock'

Edith, aged about four

Family friend: 'What are you going to be when you are grown up,
little girl?'
Edith: 'A genius.'

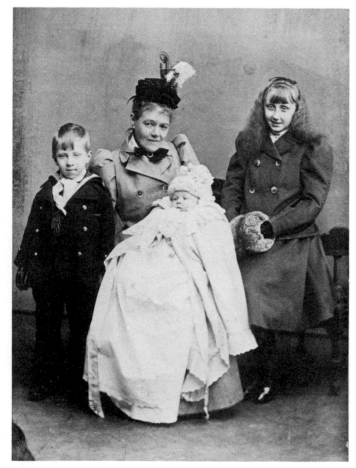

(*above left*) Osbert Sitwell, aged about three

Osbert was Lady Ida's favourite child.
'My birth caused Edith to be relegated to a second place in the nursery, a position which her very nature forbade her to occupy even at that tender age . . . in consequence it was only a few months after my birth that this little creature tried to run away from home.' Osbert Sitwell, *Left Hand, Right Hand!*

(*above right*) Sacheverell Sitwell, aged about three

'A particularly fascinating and genial child . . . his love of life and of people was so intense that . . . he would often run up to strangers and say to them, "My Mummy and Daddy would be delighted if you would lunch with them tomorrow." ' Osbert Sitwell, *Left Hand, Right Hand!*

Edith, aged eleven, with her brothers Osbert and Sacheverell and their nurse Davis

'. . . life seemed less a stranger, then,
Than ever after in this cold existence.'

Edith Sitwell, 'Colonel Fantock'

The garden at Renishaw, entrance to 'The Wilderness'

Life was so still, so clear, that to wake
Under a kingfisher's limpid lake
In the lovely afternoon of a dream
Would not remote or stranger seem.
Everything seemed so clear for a while—
The turn of a head or a deep-seen smile;
Then a smile seen through wide leaves or deep water,
That beauty seemed to the King's daughter;
For a flying shadow passed, then gone
Was the gleam, and the Princess was alone.

How sweet seemed the flowers of spring again—
As pink as Susan and Polly and Jane,
Like country maids so sweet and shy
Who bloom and love and wonder not why:
Now when summer comes it seems the door
To the graves that lie under the trival floor,
And the gardens hard to touch and shining,
Where no mirage dew lies whining.
And the sweet flowers seem for a fading while
Dear as our first love's youthful smile—
Till they bruise and wound the heart and sense
With their lost and terrible innocence.

Edith Sitwell, *The Sleeping Beauty*, Canto 9

The garden at Renishaw, viewed from the statues of the 'Giants'.
Photograph by Reresby Sitwell.

'The garden at Renishaw and the great lake below are the creations of Sir George Sitwell and are a fitting memorial to his skill and taste. The yew hedges and pyramids begin on either side of the lawn in front of the house . . . he installed a pair of marble fountains and various statues—the two best are Diana and Neptune by Caligari', the two nearest to the house. The other pair are known as the Giants. Reresby Sitwell, *Renishaw Hall and the Sitwells*

(*opposite*) *Sir George and Lady Ida Sitwell with their children Edith, Osbert and Sacheverell*
Oil painting by John Singer Sargent. 1900–01. Collection of the Sitwell Settled Estates.

'When I was about twelve years old, my father determined that He (I must really use a capital letter in this connection) must be portrayed for posterity . . . After a good deal of fussing, he decided that Sargent was to be the artist whom he would take under his wing, and he set about teaching the gentleman in question his business.

'My father was portrayed in riding-dress (he never rode), my mother in a white-spangled low evening gown and a hat with feathers, arranging, with one prettily shaped, flaccid, entirely useless hand, red anemones in a silver bowl (she never arranged flowers, and in any case it would have been a curious occupation for one wearing a ball-dress, even if, at the same time, she wore a hat).

'The colour of the anemones was repeated in my scarlet dress. I was white with fury and contempt, and indignant that my father held me in what he thought was a tender paternal embrace. Osbert and Sacheverell, sitting on the floor, playing with my mother's black pug were the only beings that seemed to have any trace of life.'
Edith Sitwell, *Taken Care Of*

Renishaw Hall, from the stable gate. Photograph by Reresby Sitwell.

'The ancient building straddles the crest of a hill; the approach drive winds up through parkland past gaunt old trees that stand sentinel around the entrance front.' Reresby Sitwell, *Renishaw Hall and the Sitwells*

(*opposite*) *Edith Sitwell*
Oil painting by Roger Fry. 1918. Sheffield City Art Galleries, Sheffield.

'I knew the painter and distinguished art critic, Roger Fry, well for I sat to him for several portraits. For one of these I wore a green evening dress, the colour of the leaves of lilies, and my appearance in this, in the full glare of the midsummer light of midday, in Fitzroy Square, together with the appearance of Mr. Fry, his bushy long grey hair floating from under an enormous black sombrero, caused great joy to the children of the district as we crossed from Mr. Fry's studio to his house for luncheon.

'Imagining us to be stray revellers, they enquired at moments (perhaps not unnaturally) if our mothers knew we were out. At other moments they referred to the fifth of November [Guy Fawkes' Day], when according to them, our appearance would have been better timed.' Edith Sitwell, *Taken Care Of*

The Great Drawing-room with the Sargent portrait

'The Great Drawing-room was built ... in 1803 and is nearly 70 feet long with seven huge windows ... The main feature of this room is the magnificent commode, attributed to the designs of Robert Adam and the workmanship of Thomas Chippendale ... and above this hangs the celebrated conversation piece by John Singer Sargent of Sir George Sitwell, his wife Lady Ida and their three famous children ...' Reresby Sitwell, *Renishaw Hall and the Sitwells*

'When I stepped inside the house after the train and the dust of the hot August day, I saw tapestry, inlaid cabinets and velvet and gold chairs from a palace in Venice; paintings and little vines in pots, coolness and space. There were tall vases full of pink roses set in front of the blue-green tapestry and the whole room was suffused by their fragrance.' Constance Sitwell, *Bright Morning*

Wood End, Scarborough. Gouache and ink drawing by John Piper. 1942. Collection of Scarborough Borough Council

'Dark and forgotten and a little precious, like an unopened seventeenth-century first edition in a library.' Edith Sitwell, 'Readers and Writers'.

'I was always a little outside life.'

Edith Sitwell, 'Colonel Fantock'

Edith (in a dark skirt, centre) at the art class, Scarborough

'Having discovered that I had no talent whatsoever for the pictorial arts [my father] determined that I should be forced to learn to draw at the local Art School, which specialised in a damping-down process of an extraordinary proficiency... [The drawing mistress] did not hate art, she simply ignored it...' Edith Sitwell, *Taken Care Of*

Edith, aged about seventeen

'. . . with my face remorselessly "softened" by my hair being frizzed and then pulled down over my nose I resembled a caricature of the Fairy Queen in a pantomime.' Edith Sitwell, 'A Self-developed Person'

(*top*) Osbert, aged about seventeen

(*above*) Sacheverell, aged about eleven

LONDON

'It was proper for a gently brought up young girl to leave her family provided that she was suitably chaperoned. With Helen Rootham as a buffer against the charge of impropriety, Edith Sitwell escaped from the suffocation of parental disapproval and rented a cheap flat in Bayswater on the fourth floor of Pembridge Mansions. Miss Sitwell had come to London.'

Elizabeth Salter and Allanah Harper, Fire of the Mind

Roger Fry

'Mr. Fry was a most delightful companion...Warm-hearted, generous-minded and kindly, he was always espousing some lost cause, championing some unfortunate person, rushing at some windmill with a lance.'   Edith Sitwell, *Taken Care Of*

W. B. Yeats

Yeats, like Swinburne, was a passion of Edith's adolescence. 'I once left red roses on his doorstep. I ran away quickly before anyone opened the door but I think he knew who had left them!'   Edith Sitwell to the author

T. S. Eliot

T. S. Eliot was declared by Edith Sitwell to be 'one of the greatest [poets] of the last one hundred and fifty years'; he had 'flooded himself with the immediate age as with vast oceanic tides'. In appearance, she said, he was a 'shy creature, always very carefully dressed. I do hate romantic wanderers who are too great spirits to be in the city. Tom Eliot was a bank clerk for ages and is still a publisher!' Edith Sitwell to the author

Virginia Woolf

'Virginia Woolf had a moonlit transparent beauty. She was exquisitely carved, with large thoughtful eyes that held no foreshadowing of that tragic end which was a grief to everyone who had ever known her.' Edith Sitwell, *Taken Care Of*

41

Alvaro Guevara

Alvaro Guevara was the first acknowledged love of Edith's life. 'He is tall and muscular with the physique of an athlete; but he wore the absent expression of one who searches for some elusive and subtle truth.' Silva Vildosola, 1918, quoted by Diana Holman Hunt, *Latin Among Lions*

Roy Campbell

'I have never known a more vitalising companion ... Of great stature, build, strength, and vitality, he had eyes of the flashing blue of the kingfisher.' Edith Sitwell, *Taken Care Of*

Self- portrait
Oil painting by Alvaro Guevara. 1924. Collection of Mr. and Mrs. Donn Davies, Taos, New Mexico.

According to his sister, Guevara painted this portrait of himself, dressed as a cowboy, for fun.

Alvaro Guevara

'In the London art world Jacob Kramer, Chile [Guevara] and myself were the three best fighters by a long way, though Chile only developed his full strength when he was quite old . . . in the end he only lost to Godoy in the whole of South America.' Roy Campbell, 1919, quoted by Diana Holman Hunt, *Latin Among Lions*

Frontispiece design for *Wheels*
Gouache by Gino Severini. 1920. Private collection.

'When Mr. Eliot, my brothers and I began to publish our poems, certain newspapers turned from their healthy and, to me, extremely exciting interest in crime and focused their attention on us.' Edith Sitwell, quoted by Elizabeth Salter, *The Last Years of a Rebel*

Above right Wilfred Owen

The young poet Wilfred Owen was killed in 1918 and his work was first published by Edith Sitwell in the edition of *Wheels* for 1919, which was dedicated to him as 'the greatest poet of our time'.

Aldous Huxley

Huxley was a lifelong friend of Edith Sitwell and an early contributor to *Wheels*. She described him as 'tall, with hair the colour of the earth, given to silences, but one of the best talkers I have ever known—especially if uninterrupted.' On the subject of his later experiments with mescalin she refused to be drawn but, she said, 'no poet should need a drug to produce extreme sensibility, which must be, if he is any good, a part of his equipment.' Elizabeth Salter, *The Last Years of a Rebel*

Cecil Beaton

Cecil Beaton's series of Sitwell photographs in the early 1920s was
unusual enough to attract attention to the photographer as well as
to his subjects.

Edith Sitwell at Renishaw. Photograph by Cecil Beaton.

'I have my own particular elegance, but I am as stylised as the music of Debussy or Ravel.' Edith Sitwell quoted by Elizabeth Salter, *The Last Years of a Rebel*

(opposite)

Edith Sitwell in repose. Photograph by Cecil Beaton.

This was one of Edith Sitwell's favourite portraits of herself.

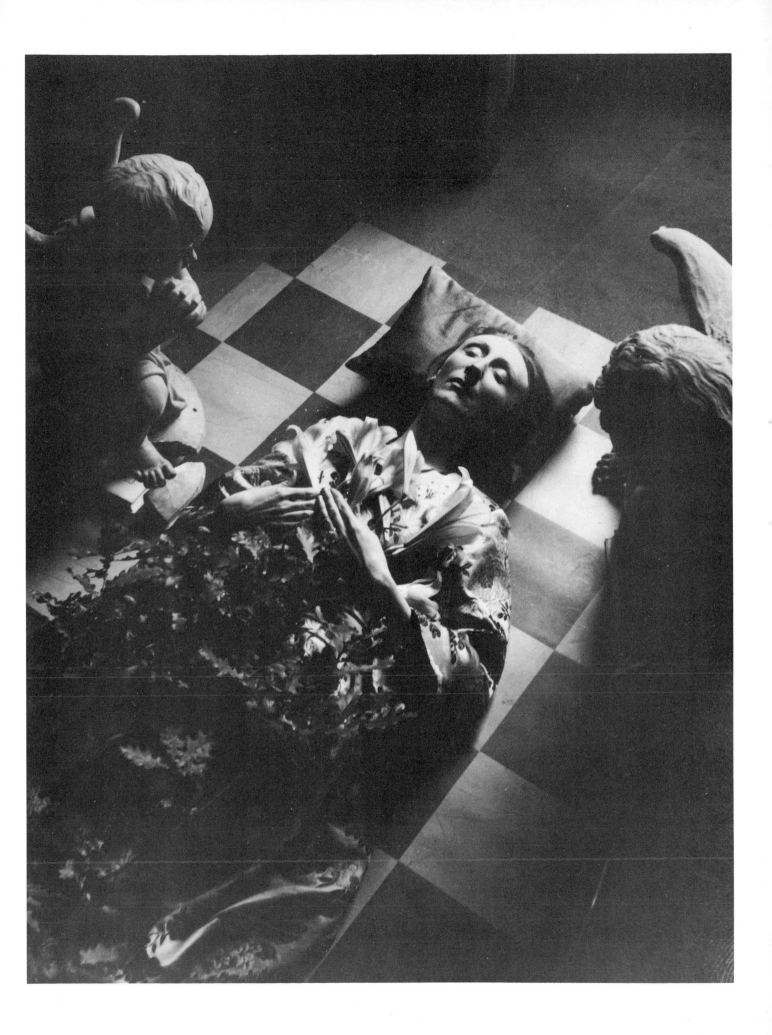

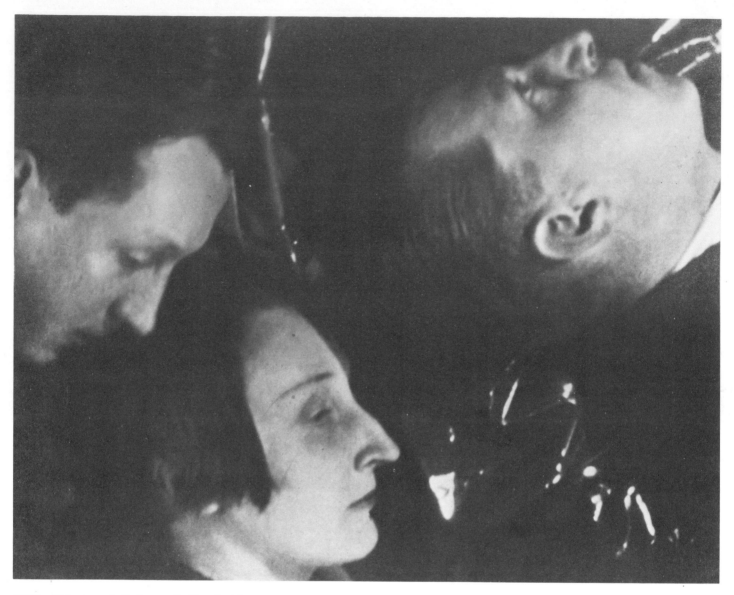

Edith, Osbert and Sacheverell Sitwell. Photograph by Cecil
Beaton.

'The vanguard of British poetry. They are a portent'. *The Saturday
Review*

(*opposite*) *Edith, Osbert and Sacheverell Sitwell*
Ink drawing by Cecil Beaton. Humanities Research Center,
University of Texas, Austin.

'This latter-day Plantagenet who, with the help of her brothers
Osbert and Sacheverell, had draped her six feet of slender bone
structure with brocades decorated by semi-precious jewels, like a
tall tree in flower.' Elizabeth Salter and Allanah Harper, *Fire of the
Mind*

49

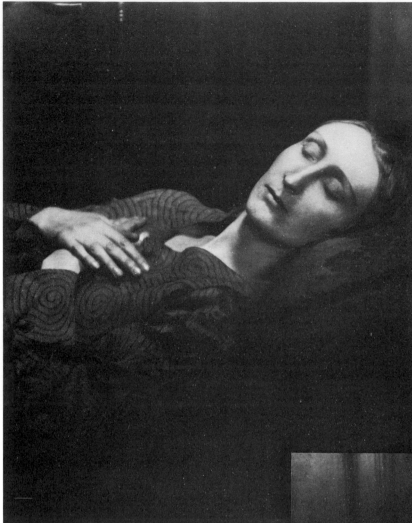

(*opposite*) *The Editor of 'Wheels'*
Oil painting by Alvaro Guevara. 1919. Tate Gallery, London.

'With Guevara Edith formed one of the two most important relationships of her life... For the second edition of *Wheels*, Alvaro contributed a design for end-papers based on his oil-painting *Trickcyclists*. But the important memorial to his friendship with Edith is his portrait of her which was first exhibited in the autumn of 1919 and which stylistically was probably executed earlier that year. The upward-tilted perspective gives added drama to the composition that shimmers with bright colour, whilst Edith sits on an Omega chair, her eyes half-closed, withdrawn into her self and oblivious of her appearance and her brilliant surroundings. On seeing this picture the poet Gordon Bottomley wrote to the painter John Nash: "I like Edith the best of the Sitwells; her impudences charm me; and I adore her portrait by Guevara"'. Frances Spalding, 'Poet among Painters', *Images of Edith*

(*above and right*) Edith Sitwell. Photographs by Maurice Beck.

'A hieratic figure in Limoges enamel ... the pale oval face with its almond eyes and long thin nose has often been carved in ivory by believers. Her entire figure possessed a distinction seldom to be seen outside the glass cases of certain museums.' Harold Acton, *Selected Letters*

Nellie Wallace

Edith Sitwell's favourite music-hall entertainer was Nellie Wallace, whose appeal to her slightly denuded feather boa she was to quote at appropriate moments: 'For God's sake hold together boys!'

Music-hall
Pencil and chalk drawing by Walter Sickert. Private collection.

Sickert's *Music-hall* was one of Edith Sitwell's treasured possessions which, she said, resulted from the following conversation:
'Friend: "This woman admires your pictures."
Sickert: "Either she is mad or very intelligent. Which are you?"
Edith: "Mad."
Sickert was so delighted that he gave me the picture.'

(*opposite*) *Edith Sitwell*
Oil painting by Rex Whistler. Early 1920s. Collection of Reresby Sitwell.

'Except for her hands, she insisted that she had no beauty. She disliked the word "plain"; she thought of herself as ugly. The secret of her appearance, she explained, lay in the fact that she was as stylish as possible.'

Elizabeth Salter, *The Last Years of a Rebel*

Frontispiece design for *Façade*
Gouache by Gino Severini. 1919. Private collection.

' "How did *Façade* come about?", I asked.
"It was a kind of dare. Willie gave me different rhythms and said, 'here you are Edith, see what you can do with that.' " ' Edith Sitwell to the author

William Walton, Photograph by Cecil Beaton.

William Walton's genius was recognized at Oxford by his fellow student Sacheverell Sitwell and he became a protégé of all three Sitwells. It was while they were living in Osbert Sitwell's house in Carlyle Square that *Façade* came about. A private performance was given in the home of Mrs. Robert Mathias, patron of Les Ballets Russes, the speakers using the sengerphone behind a curtain designed by Frank Dobson.

Osbert, Edith and Sacheverell Sitwell, William Walton and Neil Porter at the Chenil Galleries, London in 1926.

Edith Sitwell and Neil Porter rehearsing for the performance of *Façade* on the same occasion

'The first public performance of *Façade* [in the Aeolian Hall, London, in 1923] raised an uproar among such custodians of the purity of our language as writers of Revue, firemen on duty at the hall and passing postmen who, on being lassoed and consulted by journalists, expressed the opinion that we were mad' (Edith Sitwell quoted by Elizabeth Salter, *The Last Years of a Rebel*). But when it was revived at the Chenil Galleries Ernest Newman wrote, 'Here is obviously a humorous musical talent of the first order, nothing so good in the mock-serious line had been heard for a long time . . . At its best, *Façade* was the jolliest entertainment of the season.'

MS of the Waltz from *Façade*
Private collection.

So Daisy and Lily,
Lazy and silly,
Walk by the shore of the wan grassy sea,
Talking once more 'neath a swan-bosomed tree.
Rose castles,
Tourelles,
Those bustles!
Mourelles
Of the shade in their train follow.
Ladies, how vain,—hollow,—
Gone is the sweet swallow,—
Gone, Philomel!

SITWELLIAN FEUDS

'Having in many ways a feline nature, it amuses her to sharpen her wits upon the wooden heads of her adversaries as much as it amuses a cat to sharpen his claws upon the leg of a table.
And nearly all her battles are the result of this, or of her rather outrageous sense of fun. She has never wished to wound, and hopes her adversaries are getting an equal amount of fun out of the battle.'

Edith Sitwell, 'That English Eccentric Edith Sitwell'

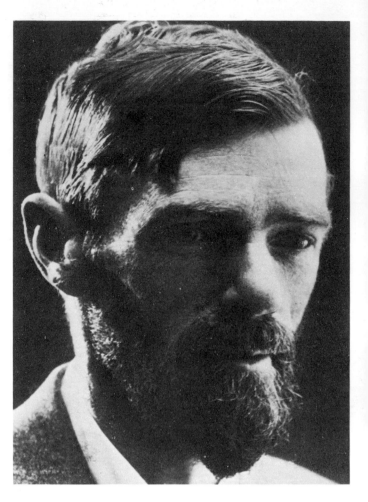

(*above left*) Noël Coward

The first public performance of *Façade* was the inspiration for a series of sketches Noël Coward was later to write, lampooning the Sitwells as 'The Swiss Family Whittlebot'. The result was a forty-year feud brought to an end through the intervention of the film director George Cukor, a mutual friend who arranged for Coward to visit Edith Sitwell in her London flat in 1962. After this they were the best of friends.

(*above right*) D. H. Lawrence

D. H. Lawrence was a target for attack after the publication of *Lady Chatterley's Lover*, for which Edith Sitwell believed her family and her home were prototypes. It was an opinion later borne out by a request from a film company to use Renishaw as a background for a film based on the book, a request refused with indignation. 'I am not and never will be interested in the goings-on on Monkey Hill.'

(*left*) Wyndham Lewis

Wyndham Lewis described himself as 'Edith's favourite enemy'. 'This remarkable man . . . had a habit of appearing in various roles, partly as a disguise and partly in order to defy his own loneliness. There was the Spanish role, for instance, in which he would assume a gay, if sinister manner, very masculine and gallant, and deeply impressive to a feminine observer. When appearing in this character he would wear a sombrero and, from time to time, would allow the expression 'Carramba!' to escape him . . .' Edith Sitwell, *Taken Care Of*

(*opposite*) *Edith Sitwell*
Pencil and watercolour by Wyndham Lewis. 1922–28. Cecil Higgins Gallery, Bedford.

'I sat [for Wyndham Lewis] every day excepting Sundays for ten months . . . In his enormous studio mice emerged from their holes and lolled against the furniture, staring in the most insolent way at the sitter . . . so Lewis bought a large gong which he placed near the mousehole and, when matters reached a certain limit, he would strike this loudly and the mice would retreat.' Edith Sitwell in a letter to the author

(*above left*) *Edith Sitwell*
Pencil drawing by Wyndham Lewis. 1921. Private collection.

(*above right*) *Edith Sitwell*
Pencil drawing by Wyndham Lewis. 1923. National Portrait Gallery, London.

(*left*) *Edith Sitwell*
Pencil drawing by Powys Evans. Humanities Research Center, University of Texas, Austin.

(*opposite*) *Edith Sitwell*
Lead (?) bust by Frank Dobson. Collection of Reresby Sitwell.

61

PARIS

'My life there was unmitigated hell.'

Edith Sitwell, Taken Care Of

The rue Saint-Dominique. Photograph by Paula Davies.

The flat in the rue Saint-Dominique on the first floor, with the balcony just visible in this photograph, became Edith Sitwell's retreat when her London fame brought too many interruptions to her work. Her contempt for fashionable society and her refusal to be 'lionized' is best illustrated by the following letter, quoted in Osbert Sitwell's *Left Hand, Right Hand!*

'Dear Mrs. Almer,
After five years you have again been kind enough to ask me to luncheon. The reason for this is that I have just published a successful book: the reason I have had a successful book is that I do not go out and waste my time and energy, but work hard, morning and afternoon. If I accept your kind invitation, I shall have to leave off earlier in the morning, and shall be too tired to work in the afternoon. Then my next book will not be such a success and you will not ask me to luncheon; or at the best, less often. So that, under these circumstances, I am sure you will agree it is wiser for me not to accept your present kind invitation.

Yours sincerely,
Edith Sitwell.'

Interior of the flat in the rue Saint-Dominique. Photograph by Paula Davies.

This photograph shows the flat as it was when the author visited it in 1959, twenty years after Edith Sitwell had left it. Her books and her collection of Tchelitchew paintings had been carefully preserved, some stored in a cupboard papered over to conceal it from the Germans during the occupation but discovered by the author.

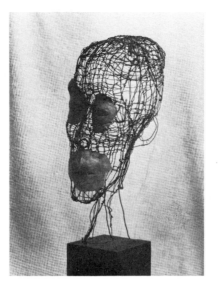

(*above*) Pavel Tchelitchew. Photograph by Carl van Vechten.

(*above centre*) *Self-portrait.*
Wax and wire sculpture by Pavel Tchelitchew. 1929. Private collection.

'He executed a sculpture of my head in wax on wire, one of his three only sculptures ... I own one in the same medium called 'The Clown', a most tragic work which is, actually, a self-portrait.' Edith Sitwell, *Taken Care Of*

(*above right*) Pavel Tchelitchew. Photograph by George Platt Lynes.

The Russian-born painter with whom Edith Sitwell fell in love came to Paris to design a ballet for Diaghilev's Ballets Russes.

Tchelitchew was 'discovered' by Stein and later migrated to the United States where he achieved international recognition.

'Could we foretell the worm within the heart,
That holds the households and the parks of heaven,
Could we foretell that land was only earth,
Would it be worth the pain of death and birth,
Would it be worth the soul from body riven?

'For here, my sight, my sun, my sense,
In my gown white as innocence
I walked with you. Ah, that my sun
Loved my heart less than carrion!'

Edith Sitwell, 'The Hambone and the Heart'
(dedicated to Tchelitchew)

(*right*) *Edith Sitwell*
Pen and ink drawing by Pavel Tchelitchew. 1932. Private collection.

'Nobody has ever understood you better or come closer to you than I have—ours is a friendship that has neither beginning nor end and which brings me enormous happiness and a limitless feeling of tenderness.' Pavel Tchelitchew in a letter to Edith Sitwell

(*opposite*) *Edith Sitwell, Gertrude Stein and Marianne Moore*
Gouache by Z. Czermanski. Humanities Research Center, University of Texas, Austin.

Gertrude Stein presided over the celebrated 'salon' in the rue de Fleurus at which Edith Sitwell met Pavel Tchelitchew. Considering her to be one of the most important influences of her day, Edith arranged for Gertrude Stein to lecture at Oxford. At a party in Pembridge Mansions she introduced Stein to Virginia Woolf, but the meeting was not a success. Indeed, Virginia Woolf wrote to Roger Fry in 1925, 'We are lying crushed under a manuscript of Gertrude Stein's. I cannot brisk myself up to deal with it—whether her contortions are genuine and fruitful, or only such spasms as we might all go through in sheer impatience at having to deal with English prose. Edith Sitwell says she's gigantic, (meaning not the flesh but the spirit). For my own part I wish we could skip a generation...'

MISS EDITH SITWELL PRESENTS A GENIUS?

Her Eulogistic Comments on a Young Russian Artist

M. Paul Tchelitchew's portrait of Miss Sitwell, who hails him as "a really great painter"

Portrait of M. Jacques Stettner. "Great and, at first glance, slightly terrifying works of art," says Miss Sitwell

A Poem by Miss Edith Sitwel.
Said King Pompey, the em-
peror's ape,
Shuddering black in his tem-
poral cape
Of dust: "The dust is
everything—
The heart to love and the
voice to sing,
Indianapolis,
And the Acropolis,
Also the hairy sky that we
Take for a coverlet comfort-
ably." . . .
Said the Bishop
Eating his ketchup—
"There still remains Eternity
(Swelling the diocese)—
That elephantiasis
The flunkeyed and trumpet-
ing sea !"
(By permission of Messrs. Duckworth)

"These works are full of surprises."
Another portrait of Miss Sitwell

M. Paul Tchelitchew, whom Miss Edith Sitwell here eulogizes, is holding an exhibition at the Claridge Galleries. He designed the decor for the new Russian Ballet, "Ode." We publish her unqualified eulogy without comment :

LONDON has been introduced to a really great new painter, Paul Tchelitchew. And when I say he is a really great painter, I mean what I say. He is not one of these new sensation-mongers that crop up every year, but a painter of the greatest powers, utterly individual, and his work has both majesty and beauty.

Monsieur Tchelitchew's whole attitude towards his art has the same quality as his work—one of great and reticent dignity. Here is no clamouring at the door of the booth ; here are no somersaults to attract the crowd, and here is no yielding spirit. In the place of these forms of cowardice we have great and, at the first glance, slightly terrifying works of art—terrifying because of their silence, of their extraordinary majesty. At first, these paintings have the quality of strangeness. But after a while we become increasingly convinced of their very great beauty.

I can say with honesty that the day on which I first began to realize these pictures was one of the most important days in my artistic life. They opened out to me a whole new world of revelation and beauty, since these works are full of surprises. I have not yet seen any picture of Monsieur Tchelitchew's which did not tell one something new about an object which we have seen a thousand times, yet have never really seen. As a certain critic wrote of these pictures— I am translating his remarks with my own terms, since I have mislaid the essay in which it occurred—what at first appears as subtlety soon takes on the aspect of sublimity.   EDITH SITWELL

Portrait of Mme L. " These pictures opened out to me a whole new world of beauty," says Miss Sitwell

Tchelitchew and Edith Sitwell on holiday together in Toulon, 1931.

'Tell me honestly, do you think I dare (being as aged as I am) stay for three or four days in Milan on the way home, with the Boyar [Tchelitchew] staying at another hotel and go sight-seeing with him? Or do you think my "good name" would be gone for ever more?'
Edith Sitwell, aged forty, in a letter to her cousin Veronica Gilliat

Edith Sitwell with two portraits of her by Pavel Tchelitchew, reproduced from *The News Chronicle*, 1 October 1937

MISS
EDITH
SITWELL

" is her own master, and her book has no parallel in any literature "

(*opposite*) Edith Sitwell's article introducing Pavel Tchelitchew's art to the London art world, reproduced from *The Graphic*, 28 July 1928.

Hands of Edith Sitwell with Mask. Oil painting by Stella Bowen. c. 1934. Collection of Reresby Sitwell.

Edith Sitwell often claimed 'My hands are my face'. Stella Bowen was the Australian-born painter and mistress of Ford Madox Ford who became a mutual friend of Tchelitchew and Edith Sitwell. She handled an unhappy situation with understanding and her portraits of Edith reflect the sadness of her subject.

(opposite) Edith Sitwell
Pastel by Christopher Nevinson. c. early 1920s. Private collection.

'She has a very long expressive face with a pale but good complexion. She looks rather like a refined Dutch medieval madonna.'
Brian Howard quoted by Elizabeth Salter and Allanah Harper, *Fire of the Mind*

(page 70) Edith Sitwell. Oil painting by Wyndham Lewis. 1923–25. Tate Gallery, London.

'Lewis was seized with a kind of *schwarmerei* for me. I did not respond. Eventually I had to stop sitting for him' (the reason why the portrait has no hands).   Edith Sitwell to the author

'As a result of strained relations, Lewis flitted one night with his large oil portrait of Edith and set up his easel elsewhere. The hands were left unfinished and were completed later in 1935 in facetted areas of bright colour which, stylistically, jar with the rest of the portrait. It is to be regretted that it was not completed in front of the sitter as Edith's stylization appealed to Lewis and suited his rythmic if occasionally mannered treatment of the human figure.'
Frances Spalding, 'Poet among Painters', *Images of Edith*

Edith Sitwell, 1937. Photograph by Howard Coster.
'Nobody would have guessed at the vulnerability concealed behind
that mighty shield and buckler.' Stella Bowen of Edith Sitwell

THE WAR YEARS 1939-1945

'Still falls the Rain —
Dark as the world of man, black as our loss —
Blind as the nineteen hundred and forty nails
Upon the Cross.'

Edith Sitwell, 'Still Falls the Rain'

(*above*) Edith and Osbert Sitwell at Renishaw

Now, free of parental domination, Edith Sitwell found an atmosphere at Renishaw conducive to poetry. The result was a second flowering described by Kenneth Clark as 'a true poetic and prophetic cry which had not been heard in English since the death of Yeats'.

(*right*) Benjamin Britten

'Listening to Ben's setting of "Still Falls the Rain" I relived the awful experience of having written it.' Edith Sitwell to the author

(*top*) *Renishaw Hall*
Drawing by Rex Whistler. Collection of Reresby Sitwell.

(*above*) *Renishaw Hall*
Gouache and ink drawing by John Piper. 1939. Scarborough Borough Council, Scarborough.

'Grey and machicolated, this grim northern façade is of immense length and decidedly 'Gothick' character, concealing the narrow width of the house and the beautiful garden beyond.' Reresby Sitwell, *Renishaw Hall and the Sitwells*

'The poem ['The Shadow of Cain'] came into being thus. On the 10th of September, 1945, nearly five weeks after the fall of the first atom bomb, my brother Sir Osbert Sitwell and I were in the train going to Brighton, where we were to give a reading. He pointed out to me a paragraph in The Times, *a description by an eye witness of the immediate effect of the atomic bomb upon Hiroshima. That witness saw a totem pole of dust arise to the sun as a witness against the murder of mankind . . . A totem pole, the symbol of creation, the symbol of generation.'*

Edith Sitwell, preface to Collected Poems

(*above left*) Dylan Thomas

Dylan Thomas's work was discovered by Edith Sitwell in 1935 when he was twenty-one years old and looked, she said, 'like a youthful Silenus if Rubens had taken it into his head to paint him'. 'His voice resembles no other voice, the spirit is that of the beginning of created things; there is here no case of separate imagination, or invention. From the depths of Being, from the roots of the world, a voice speaks.' Edith Sitwell's review of Dylan Thomas's *Collected Poems* (1953)

(*above right*) Jack Lindsay

Jack Lindsay is the Australian-born historian and critic whose review of 'The Shadow of Cain' brought Edith Sitwell much-needed encouragement.

(*left*) Humphrey Searle

Searle's setting of 'The Shadow of Cain' was first performed at the Palace Theatre, London, with Edith Sitwell and Dylan Thomas as readers.

Edith Sitwell at Renishaw. Photograph by Bill Brandt.

'I wrote of the summer of the earth and of the heart, and how the warmth of the heart faded and only a false brotherhood remained.' Edith Sitwell of her own poetry

AMERICA

'How much I do like the Americans — anyone who doesn't must be mad.'

Edith Sitwell in a letter to John Lehmann, 6 January 1949

Celebrity at a Cocktail.
Watercolour cartoon by Keogh. Humanities Research Center, University of Texas, Austin.

On 19 November 1948, the arrival of the Sitwells in New York was celebrated with a 'party to end all parties' at the Gotham Book Mart: '"...the darndest assortment of celebrities, freaks, refugees from Park Lane," and the lifted-eberhart" Gore Vidal and José couldn't make my way from the tea table to the alcove where Miss Sitwell sat—pining for a cup of tea.' Frances Steloff, 'Some Gotham Party Lines'

The Gotham Book Mart Party

In the left foreground is William Rose Benet, behind him Stephen Spender and behind Spender are Horace Gregory and his wife Maria Zwalenska. Seated behind the Sitwells are, left to right, Tennessee Williams, Richard Eberhart, Gore Vidal and José Garcia Villa. On the ladder is W. H. Auden. Standing over against the bookcase, on the right, is Elizabeth Bishop and seated in front, Marianne Moore. Seated at the right is Randall Jarrell, with the moustache, and Delmore Schwartz, while Charles (Henri) Ford is in the centre, on the floor.

Edith and Osbert Sitwell on a lecture tour of the United States, 1948–49

Edith and Osbert Sitwell in Hollywood, 1951

Edith Sitwell's 1948 tour of the United States was the first of many. In 1951 she found herself in Hollywood invited to give a reading of the sleep-walking scene from *Macbeth*. 'Queen Edith' wore a crown for the occasion which, she reported, was a 'great success'.

'Lots of filmstars, including Harpo Marx came ... I was just announcing that Hell is murky when a poor gentleman in the audience uttered the most piercing shrieks and was carried out by four men, foaming at the mouth. ... I got into a Laocöon entanglement with Miss Mary Pickford [who] discoursed to me of her role as Little Lord Fauntleroy and said she had always regarded herself as a Spiritual Beacon. We also met Miss Ethel Barrymore who was delightful, although Osbert ascribes my bronchitis to her as she was breathing heavily—I must say I couldn't have enjoyed Hollywood more.' Edith Sitwell in a letter to John Lehmann, 17 January 1951

(*opposite*) Edith Sitwell giving a reading in the United States

Edith Sitwell in the sleep-walking scene in *Macbeth*.
Photographs by George Platt Lynes.

Lady Macbeth. Out, damned spot! out, I say! — One; two: why,
then 'tis time to do't. — Hell is murky. — Fie, my Lord, fie! a soldier
and afeared? — What need we fear who knows it, when none can
call our power to accompt? — Yet who would have thought the old
man to have had so much blood in him?

Doctor. Do you mark that?

Lady Macbeth. The Thane of Fife had a wife: where is she now? —
What, will these hands ne'er be clean? — No more 'o that, my Lord,
no more 'o that: you mar all with this starting.

Doctor. Go to, go to: you have known what you should not.

Gentlewoman. She has spoke what she should not, I am sure of that:
Heaven knows what she has known.

Lady Macbeth. Here's the smell of the blood still: all the perfumes
of Arabia will not sweeten this little hand. Oh! oh! oh!

Macbeth, Act V, Scene 1.

THE SESAME CLUB 1957-1962

'Edith Sitwell was the most unpredictable of women. In her orbit contradictions manifested themselves as natural phenomena. The first of these, as far as I was concerned, was the Sesame Club. Perhaps the dramatic instinct that she possessed in full made her appreciate the value of contrast. By the time one had traversed the colourless foyer, the long corridor lined with chairs like the deck of a ship and occupied by old ladies who looked as if they had taken root and withered where they sat, and emerged, blinking, into the gloom of the little bar in which she entertained, the shock of coming into Edith's presence was great . . . In such a setting she looked as exotic as an orchid in a field of turnips.'

Elizabeth Salter, The Last Years of a Rebel

(*right*) Sir Alec Guinness

Friend and fellow convert to Roman Catholicism, Alec Guinness recorded in the early war years a selection of Edith Sitwell's poetry, including her first published poem, 'Serenade' (*Daily Mirror*, 1913).

'The tremulous gold of stars within your hair
Are yellow bees flown from the hive of night,
Finding the blossom of your eyes more fair
Than all the pale flowers folded from the light.
Then, Sweet, awake, and ope your dreaming eyes
Ere those bright bees have flown and darkness dies.'

(*below*) James Purdy. Photograph by Carl van Vechten

James Purdy was the American novelist who was the last of Edith's literary 'discoveries'. She described him as 'a writer of genius who, long after my death will be acclaimed as one of the greatest writers ever to come out of America'. In their correspondence Purdy wrote, 'I do want to be worthy of your tribute Dame Edith and I will spend the rest of my life writing in the hope that I may'.

(*below right*) Graham Greene

'Leprosy was, at this stage of her life, much on her mind. It had a special horror for her ... "I am horrified to hear from Graham Greene that he is intending to stay for two months in various leper colonies in the Congo," she wrote to her friend Jeanne Stonor. "Adventurousness can go too far. But I am telling him he must regard us as moral lepers and come and see us first." ' Elizabeth Salter, *The Last Years of a Rebel*

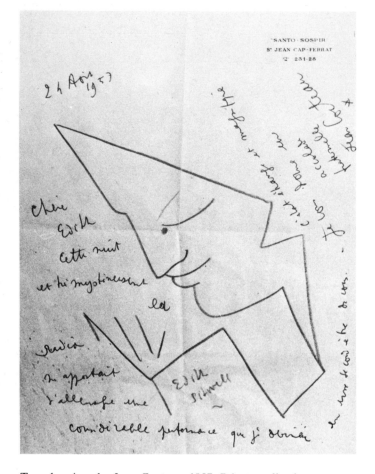
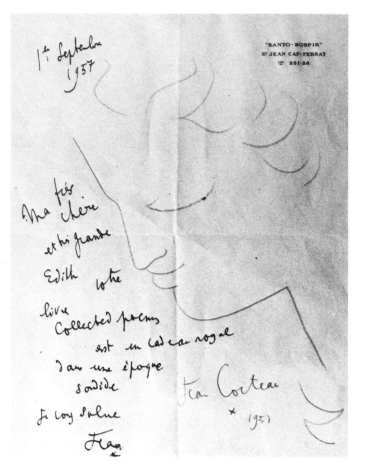

Two drawings by Jean Cocteau. 1957. Private collection.

Cocteau, who had a deep admiration for Edith Sitwell's work, wrote to her, 'Les gens ont oublié que le génie existe . . . Reste ce que vous êtes et ce que nous émerveille.'

(*opposite*) *Edith Sitwell*. Pastel by Pavel Tchelitchew. 1935. Private collection.

'A beautiful sheltered eroticism, the purely passive female sensibility that lives forever, a glass flower under glass.' Pavel Tchelitchew quoted by Parker Tyler in *The Divine Comedy of Pavel Tchelitchew*

86

Edith Sitwell
Gouache by Stanley Lench. Collection of Michael Stapleton.

Edith Sitwell
Oil painting by Feliks Topolski. 1959. Humanities Research Center, University of Texas, Austin.

'For the last time in her life she sat for an artist, visiting him at his studio under the railway arches at Hungerford Bridge. She did not however enjoy the results which she described as "an unspeakable caricature". The royal effect of the crown was offset by curvature of her spine which she thought made her look like a hunchback.' Elizabeth Salter, *The Last Years of a Rebel*.

(*opposite*) *Edith Sitwell*. Oil painting by Pavel Tchelitchew. 1937. Tate Gallery, London (on loan from the Edward James Foundation).

'William Carlos Williams on seeing one of Tchelitchew's portraits, remarked how dissimilar it appeared to the image of Edith he had obtained from her verse. "She is like that," Tchelitchew replied. "A very beautiful woman. She is alone. She is very positive and emotional. She takes herself very seriously and seems to be as cold as ice. She is not so."

'Williams's description of the picture he was looking at when Pavel said the above, does not fit any known picture of Edith, but it comes closest to the large full length executed in 1937 now in the Tate Gallery. Edith is seen holding a quill pen, wearing a severe, almost monastic gown, decorated only by the barbaric splendour of a huge amber brooch.' Frances Spalding, 'Poet among Painters,' *Images of Edith*

A. Name in full (Block letters as throughout)

....

B. Specimen of usual signature ....

C. Passport number .... (This must be accompanied by
six photographs 2½ inches by 4, and these must be signed both
by a clergyman and by a Justice of the Peace. They must, also,
have been taken within the last six months. Old photographs
cannot be accepted.

D. Finger Prints number (if any) ....

E. When were you born ....

F. Where were you born ....

G. How were you born ....

H. If not, why not ....

I. For what purpose are you going there ....

....

J. And if so, where ....

K. Of what sex are you ....

L. Age, sex and weight of your wife ....

....

M. Father's name in full ....

N. Mother's maiden name in full ....

O. Has any relative of yours ever been confined in a mental home

....

P. If not, why not ....

Q. If so, give full details, with accompanying photograph ....

....

R. Did you ever meet Burgess and Maclean, or anyone who ever
knew them ? This last must be accompanied by an attestation
taken in the presence of a Commissioner of Oaths ....

....

25a Fairfax Road,
London, N.W.6.

28th March 1956

Dear Mr. Sitwell,

Here is a copy of Dame Edith's
form. It has to be filled in in
triplicate and "answers, which will
be treated as strictly confidential,
will go to form part of the Sitwell
Report on which Dame Edith and Sir
Osbert are at present at work"!

Yours sincerely

Mary Fraser

DAME EDITH'S FORM: Insulted by
critics, dogged by lion-hunters and
pestered by cranks, she devised this
form to try and shake off those unwary
and importunate persons who from
time to time would try and inflict upon
her their own literary attempts and
manuscript outpourings

Dame Edith's form for dealing with enquiries from 'pests', with a
note written by Reresby Sitwell

Edith Sitwell once said in an interview with a reporter from *The
Daily Mail*, 'I would rather have my little joke than freeze on a
pedestal'.

(*opposite, top left*) George Cukor, James Stewart

The Hollywood film director had hoped to direct the projected film
of Edith Sitwell's *Fanfare for Elizabeth*. It was Cukor who ended
the feud between Edith Sitwell and Noël Coward.

(*opposite top right*) Cyril Connolly

During the 1950s Cyril Connolly was the literary critic for
London's *Sunday Times* and wrote of Edith Sitwell's poetry, 'When
we come to compare the collected poems of Dame Edith Sitwell
with those of Yeats or Mr. Eliot or Professor Auden, it will be found
that hers have the purest intention of any; the honey may
sometimes fail, but it is never adulterated.' Cyril Connolly,
Previous Convictions

(*opposite*) Veronica Gilliat. Photograph by Paula Davies.

Edith's cousin and lifelong friend, whose beauty was of the classical
kind that does not diminish with the passing of time. Edith admired
this quality as she admired Veronica Gilliat's dress sense, a quality
she thought lacking among English women 'who will dress as
though they have been a mouse in a previous incarnation'.
Elizabeth Salter, *The Last years of a Rebel*

(*above left*) Allanah Harper. Photograph by Leja Gorska.

Allanah Harper was one of Edith's oldest friends. It was her article on the poetry of Edith Sitwell, published in *Le Flambeau*, which introduced Edith's work to the French.

(*above right*) Jeanne Stonor, now the Dowager Lady Camoys. Photograph by Gregory Harlip.

Jeanne Stonor was another of Edith Sitwell's close friends and a fellow Roman Catholic. Their friendship began with a reading Edith gave in 1957 in aid of the restoration of the beautiful little Stonor chapel.

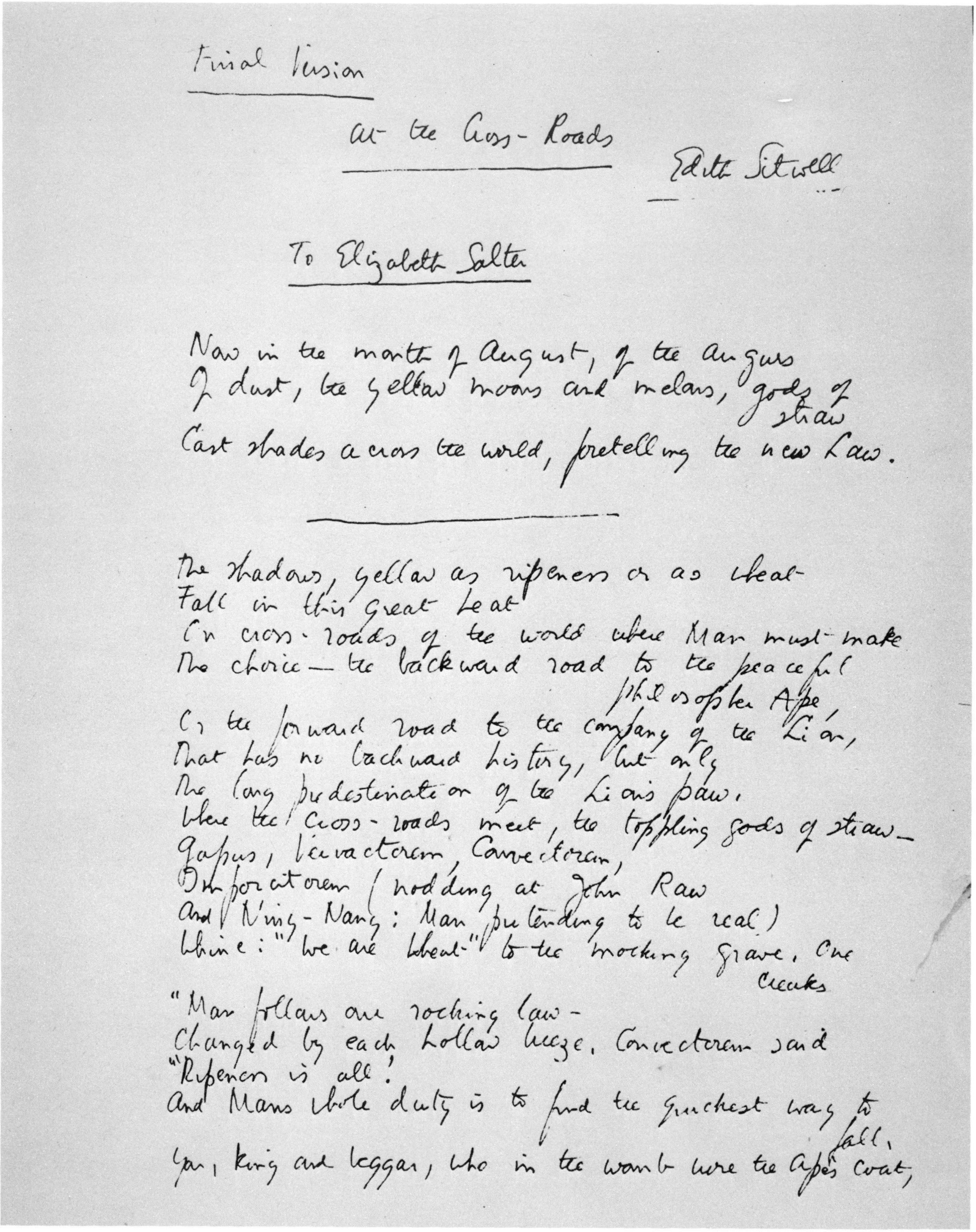

Final Version

At the Cross-Roads

Edith Sitwell

To Elizabeth Salter

Now in the month of August, of the augurs
Of dust, the yellow moons and melons, gods of straw
Cast shades across the world, foretelling the new Law.

_____

The shadows, yellow as ripeness or as wheat—
Fall in this great heat
On cross-roads of the world where Man must make
The choice — the backward road to the peaceful
                                    philosopher Ape,
Or the forward road to the company of the Lion,
That has no backward history, but only
The long predestination of the Lion's paw.
Where the Cross-roads meet, the toppling gods of straw—
Gappus, Verructorem, Convectorem,
Obturforcatorem (nodding at John Raw
And Ning-Nang: Man pretending to be real)
Whine: "We are Wheat" to the mocking grave, One
                                    creaks
"Man follows our rocking law—
Changed by each hollow breeze, Convectorem said
"Ripeness is all"
And Man's whole duty is to find the quickest way to
                                    fall,
You, King and beggar, who in the womb wore the Apes' coat,

Manuscript of 'At the Cross Roads', originally dedicated to the
author

The languno, should learn in the Ape's school
To walk on all fours, cast a longer shade to cool
The world." Another teacher squeaks
"Man's upright posture is the action of a fool!
Let him cast by the usual prejudice and stand
upon his head —
As topsy-turvy as the world; this pregnant dumb
Comment on life would bring him near to the
                                                    world's
Centre and its meaning; he would find
Himself more close to the gold within the rind
Of earth; his eyes would know more dawns; for why
Should pear-shaped Australasia have light
When we have only night!" Imporcitorem said
"If Man rejects all religion by the straw,
he must blot out history. Trust in the paw
Of the Lion that still finds nourishment in Man's
                                                    bones
that have grown dry as the bones of Tantalus
From thirst for gold; the Lion's paw will erase
The scarlet dawns of history in the veins ....
Darkness is all! ...
— So sounds the Fool's song, as he sees our planet
                                                    cool,

_____

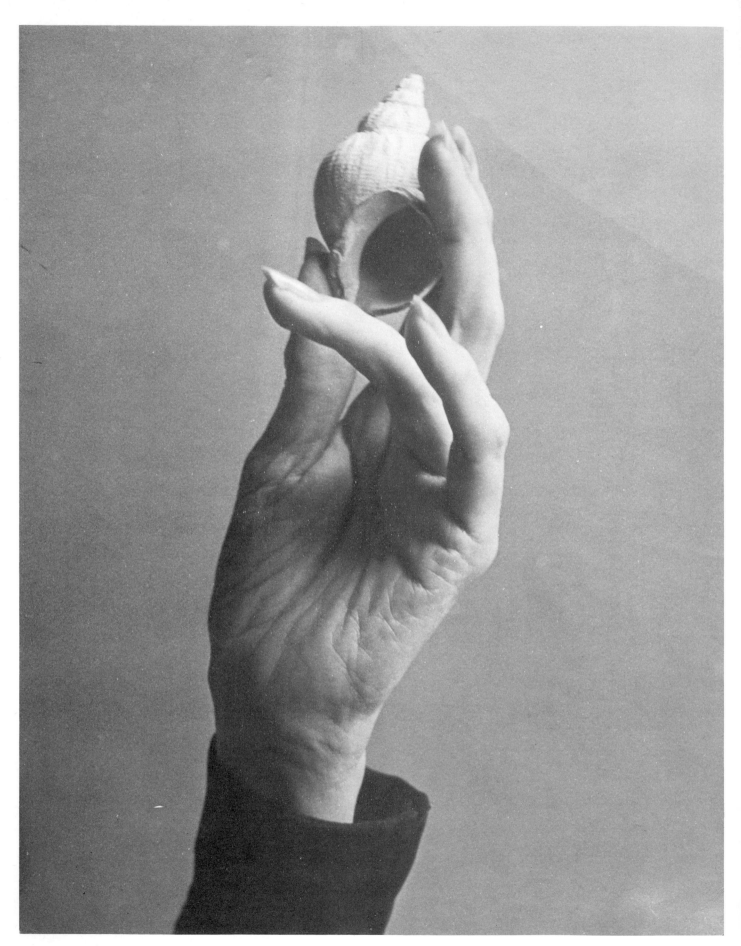

Edith Sitwell's Christmas card for 1958

This photograph was taken by Lancelot Law Whyte, a scientist and
admired friend.

(*above*) Edith Sitwell during the *Face to Face* interview with John Freeman

On 6 May 1959 Edith Sitwell was interviewed on BBC Television by John Freeman in his programme in which he brought viewers *Face to Face* with well-known personalities. In the course of the interview Edith said 'If I were to appear in the streets in a coat and skirt, people would doubt the existence of the Almighty.'

(*above right*) Leo, Edith Sitwell's beloved cat. Photograph by Mark Gerson.

'Paul Klee wrote: "I love animals. I neither lower myself to their level nor do I raise them to my own. Rather do I sink myself first of all into the whole thing and then place myself on a sort of brotherly level among neighbours—among my earthly neighbours."' Jotting in one of Edith Sitwell's notebooks

(*right*) John Freeman

John Freeman shared Edith's love of cats and sent this photograph to her at Christmas inscribed on the back with the words, 'To Dame Edith, whose cats are fit to walk with ours'.

THE LAST YEARS 1962-1964

'That lovely dying white swan, the singing sun,
Will soon be gone. But seeing the snow falling, who could tell one
From the other? The snow, that swan-plumaged circling creature, said,
"Young girl, soon the tracing of Time's bird-feet and the bird-feet of snow
Will be seen upon your smooth cheek. On, soon you will be
Colder, my sweet than me!"'

Edith Sitwell, 'A Girl's Song in Winter'

'What the reporters are like! They are mad with excitement at the
thought of my approaching demise. Kind Sister Farquhar, my nurse,
spends much of her time in throwing them downstairs. But one got in the
other day, and asked me if I mind the fact that I must die!'

Edith Sitwell in a letter to Sir John Gielgud, 3 October, 1962.

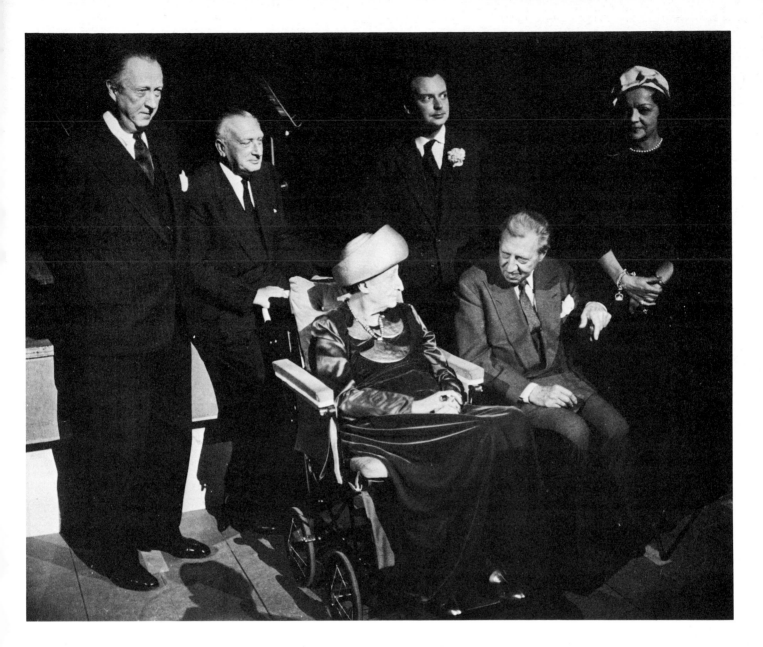

Edith Sitwell at the rehearsal for the concert in honour of her seventy-fifth birthday

From left to right are Sacheverell Sitwell, Sir William Walton, Edith Sitwell, Francis Sitwell, Osbert Sitwell and Mrs. Sacheverell Sitwell.

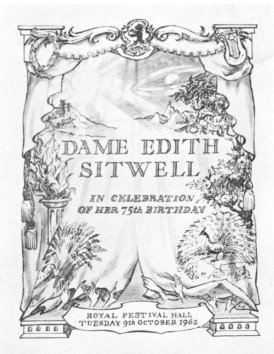

DAME EDITH SITWELL

IN CELEBRATION OF HER 75th BIRTHDAY

ROYAL FESTIVAL HALL
TUESDAY 9th OCTOBER 1962

Programme cover

Group photograph at Green Hill

Dame Edith is in the wheelchair which became the throne on which she sat to receive her guests at her Hampstead flat. From left to right are Elizabeth Salter, Lorna Coates, Edith Sitwell and Sister Farquhar.

Edith Sitwell during the performance at the Royal Festival Hall concert. She is wearing her 'Aztec' gilded collar, thought to have been specially designed for her by the Duke of Verdura, a Sicilian with a jewellery shop in New York.

This is Your Life

Amongst the many events arranged to mark Dame Edith's seventy-fifth birthday was her appearance on the BBC Television programme *This is Your Life* with Eamon Andrews on 6 November 1962. Here she is shown surrounded by her family and friends, amongst them Cecil Beaton, her brothers Osbert and Sacheverell and her nephews Francis and Reresby.

Reresby Sitwell, the present owner of Renishaw Hall.

Francis Sitwell, Edith's literary executor.

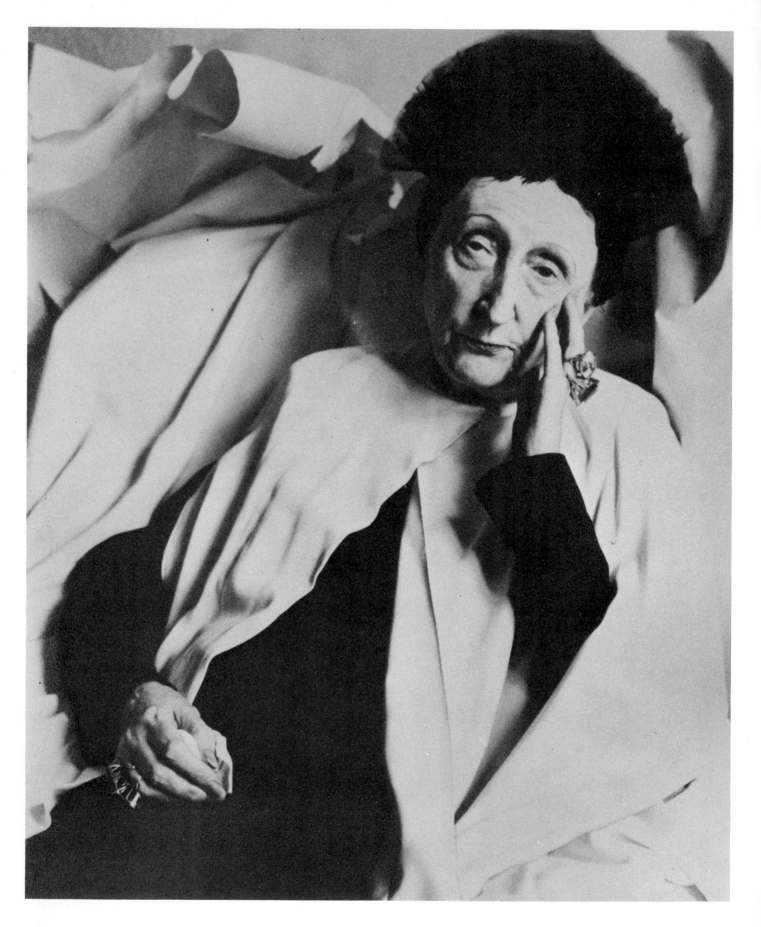

Edith Sitwell, 1962. Photograph by Cecil Beaton.

In this photograph, taken in the year of her seventy-fifth birthday,
Edith Sitwell is wearing her 'bird king's' hat.
'Why not be oneself? That is the whole secret of a successful
appearance. If one is a greyhound, why try to look like a
pekingese?' Edith Sitwell, 'Why I Look As I Do'

Edith Sitwell, 1962. Photograph by Mark Gerson.

Edith Sitwell's grave at Lois Weedon in Northamptonshire
Photograph by Reresby Sitwell.

The gravestone was designed by Henry Moore. 'A bronze plaque
set in stone depicts the hand of a young child holding the hand of an
old man to suggest the continuance of life through each generation.
An extract from " The Winds of Early Spring" was lettered in the
stone :

> The past and present are as one—
> Accordant and discordant, youth and age,
> And death and birth. For out of one came all—
> From all comes one.

Geoffrey Elborn, 'Edith Sitwell 1887–1964, A Short Biography',
Images of Edith